How to Manage Your Boss

Written by Kristie Kennard
Edited by National Press Publications

NATIONAL PRESS PUBLICATIONS
A Division of Rockhurst College Continuing Education Center, Inc.
6901 West 63rd Street • P.O. Box 2949 • Shawnee Mission, Kansas 66201-1349
1-800-258-7246 • 1-913-432-7757

National Seminars endorses nonsexist language. In an effort to make this Business User's Manual clear, consistent and easy to read, we've used "he" throughout the odd-numbered chapters and "she" throughout the even-numbered chapters. The copy is not intended to be sexist.

How to Manage Your Boss
Published by National Press Publications
A Division of Rockhurst College Continuing Education Center, Inc.
Copyright 1996 National Press Publications

Printed in the United States of America.

18 17 16 15 14

ISBN 1-55852-204-2

Table of Contents

1. Why Is Managing a Boss So Important? 1

2. Understanding How to Use Power 5

3. Assessing Yourself 17

4. Three Obstacles to Managing Your Boss 29

5. Get Smart — Get to Know Your Boss 47

6. Meeting Your Boss's Needs 69

7. Building Better Communication with Your Boss......... 81

8. Bad Bosses: What They Can Do to You
   and How You Can Stop Them 99

9. Good Bosses: What They Can Do for You
   and How You Can Manage Them 117

10. Ten Ways to Manage Your Boss 129

   Index 131

1 WHY IS MANAGING A BOSS SO IMPORTANT?

Just when you thought you had enough responsibilities at work, some-one introduces the concept of managing your boss. You say, "It's his job to manage me. Right?" Wrong.

By learning how to manage your boss, you'll not only make both your jobs easier, you'll build a personal power base that can help you get where you want to go. No matter what your position in a company, you will always have a boss.

Management is a two-way street. Subordinates must take more respon-sibility for the flow of information and feedback. The burden for manag-ing the relationship should no longer fall entirely on the boss.

It's easy for you to feel otherwise. If your boss is weak, unfocused or incompetent, you may want to avoid the relationship as much as possible. Similarly, when you're working for a boss who keeps dumping work on you, is adversarial in his attitudes or overly authoritative, it's easy to respond with passivity. Yet such attitudes are not only counterproductive, they defeat the professional image you want to project to others in your company.

What Does Managing Your Boss Mean?

It means consciously working with your boss to obtain the best possible results for the two of you and your company. The first step in mastering this process is learning how to manage yourself and take command of the situation.

Learning how to become a strong leader shows your boss two things: that you know how to take charge of yourself and that you are a dependable and trustworthy ally. Being dependable and honest with your boss creates an important professional relationship that can be a rock-solid foundation to your career and your future with the company.

Managing your boss also means you can work within the structure and gain resources, support and fair treatment. And should you have to work with others outside the chain of command, his support and influence can be invaluable.

Be aware of the four basic steps required to build a good relationship with your boss:

1. Make an honest self-appraisal of your own needs, objectives and working style.

2. Get as much detailed information as possible about your boss's goals, strengths, skills, weaknesses, preferred working style and pressures he is working under.

3. Create a relationship that fits both of your key needs and styles.

4. Take time to maintain the relationship. Keep your boss informed of your feelings and expectations, especially as they change.

Managing your boss will give you an increased awareness of your role and your boss's role — how they're the same and how they differ.

2 UNDERSTANDING HOW TO USE POWER

In the 1970s, as America began feeling the effects of stronger global competition, corporations began experimenting with a new power structure — the flattened pyramid.

If you're asking yourself, "What's this got to do with me?" the answer is "Everything!" Understanding the hierarchical nature of the corporate pyramid, its pathways of power and how they've changed is crucial to how you'll manage your boss. In this chapter we'll examine: why power pyramids exist and how they work, what kind of power your boss has and what kind of power you have.

The Power Pyramid

Whether your company has one boss and one employee or one CEO and 800 employees, there's a power pyramid at work. The big boss is at the capstone giving orders, and the employees are at the base executing them.

The pyramid as a model for modern corporate structure originates in military history. During World War II, it became the ideal way to pattern work relationships. The CEO at the top fulfilled the same role as a five-star general, and the workers at the bottom were similar to army recruits.

By tracing the job titles downward in the following list you can see how authority is delegated from one unit of authority to its logical subordinate in the corporate pyramid. Identify your job title or rank, and place yourself somewhere on this list.

- Chief Executive Officer

- President

- Executive Vice Presidents

- Senior Vice Presidents

- Vice Presidents

- Department, Regional, Product Managers

- Managerial, Zone Supervisors

- Senior Supervisors

- First-line Supervisors

- Workers

Rank and Chain of Command

The pyramid works because of two concepts: rank and the chain of command. The lower you go in the pyramid, the less powerful your level or rank.

Except for the CEO at the top and the workers at the bottom, everyone in the corporate pyramid performs the dual tasks of employee and boss. They carry out orders from their immediate boss and issue orders to the strata of employees just beneath them. This is called chain of command, and it's the lifeline that filters key information to all parts of the pyramid. It's also a vital concept underlying most interactions in today's corporate world.

The chain of command works because every employee reports to just one boss. The purpose of the pyramid is to divide both large and small tasks into manageable units that are overseen by the bosses and assembled by the employees.

Where's the Power?

Typically, the higher your rank, the more power you have. Upper-level managers, vice presidents and executive officers usually have the greatest access to a company's resources and the most responsibility for increasing those resources.

If you're an assistant to someone in upper-level management, count yourself lucky. You're automatically positioned closer to the playing field, where all the action takes place. But even if you're an employee of a boss further down in the pyramid, you still have a chance at getting in the game and wielding some power. How? Simple. By managing your boss.

Why Making Your Boss Look Good
Makes You Look Good

Aside from the substantial rewards you reap from developing a solid working relationship with your boss, managing her carries a more subtle payoff.

Most companies have two sets of rules: explicit and implicit. The *explicit* rules are the ones that are explained during the job interview or the first week on the job. They can be important: your duties, your responsibilities; or they may be trivial: when it's your turn to make coffee, where you may park.

One implicit rule is to be *proactive* rather than *reactive* in your relationship with your boss: to size up the situation at hand and quickly take responsibility.

A proactive employee doesn't wait for the boss to make every move and seeks information and the help needed to do the job. She gives the boss feedback, asks questions and initiates action without having to be supervised.

How an employee handles a boss is quite revealing, especially in the first few months of a job. Management keeps its eye on employees who show an ability to define and fulfill their own and their boss's mutual expectations in their working relationship. As opposed to those who only grumble about their bosses, management tags proactive employees as people who are "going somewhere." By learning to manage your boss well, you can attract the attention of bigger bosses and perhaps pave the way for a lateral move into the action-packed arena.

Directions: List the names of the "bosses" in your organization, starting with the highest-ranking officer. If you do not know the names of some bosses, try to get an organizational chart and fill them in later.

_____

_____

_____

_____

_____

_____

_____

_____

_____

_____

_____

Note where you are on this list.

Regardless of the size of your organization, there is a hierarchical or pyramid structure. Knowing where you are in this structure is crucial to knowing how to manage your boss.

Reflections

What Kind of Power Your Boss Has

Savvy business analysts have identified several distinct kinds of power, but basically "boss power" can be broken down into two types: the power of the position and personal power. No matter where your boss's place on the corporate pyramid, it's likely that she wields at least one kind of power. Check which ones fit your boss.

The power of the position

1. The power to reward: giving promotions, raises or recognition for a job well done

2. The power to punish: firing or transferring an employee, putting someone in charge of dead-end projects

3. Authority: can be specifically granted, like the right to sign checks, or can come with the position

Personal power

1. Expertise: being an expert, knowing a function better than anyone else in the company

2. Referent power: charm, charisma, integrity that makes others want to be like her

3. Association: who one knows, being in the right clubs and social groups, marrying the right people

The first three kinds of power come with the territory. The second three could belong to anyone at any level in the organization — a computer wizard who can handle a crashing system and get it back on line or a charming middle manager who gives speeches for local volunteer organizations.

It's rare when someone possesses all six kinds of power. Bosses are human, too — long in some suits, short in others. Often a boss who is effective and powerful in one arena does not even choose to compete in another. Probably everyone has had the experience of working for the boss's son or daughter who possesses plenty of associative power but is lacking in technical expertise. What about the highly demanding boss who threatens, challenges or competes with employees and makes no claim to personal charm? Review the "power" list above and ask yourself the following questions:

1. What kind of power does my boss possess?

2. Could she use it more effectively?

3. Can I convey that to her?

4. What kind of power does she need?

5. Can I help her get it?

It's best to keep in mind that, according to some management experts, the only real power worth having is the power of position or rank. In most corporate structures, employees quickly learn that no matter how incompetent, lazy or disorganized their boss may be, she is entitled to deference, respect and obedience because of rank and rank only. It's another one of those implicit corporate rules that complaining about your boss to her boss can constitute corporate suicide. The more hierarchical the structure of your company, the more you're expected to work with your immediate boss, to carry out her orders and be a team player. Absolute deference to your boss is the No. 1 rule.

Even if you're stuck with an incompetent boss in a highly structured company, don't despair! It may come as a surprise to you that, as an employee, you still can wield a great deal of power.

What Kind of Power You Have

Employees have the ability to make their bosses look like kings or fools. They can withhold vital information, give their bosses poor feedback or break the chain of command and route projects through other bosses.

Eventually, however, these tactics are unsuccessful and will finally catch up with their perpetrators. They demonstrate behavior that's unprofessional and demeaning to both you and your boss.

There are better ways you can "manage upward" and exercise your power in a positive manner. Let's look at some of the same types of boss power we discussed earlier and apply them to you. Identify which kinds of power you use in dealing with your boss.

The power of the position

1. The power to reward: making your boss look good, getting her out of a jam, giving her good feedback

2. The power to punish: programming your boss for failure, withholding information

3. Authority: belonging to organizations with negotiating power like labor unions, political coalitions

Personal power

1. Expertise: being a staff-level expert with a high degree of knowledge in a specialized area; knowing a function better than anyone else in the company

2. Referent power: charm, charisma, integrity that endears individuals to others; easy to talk to; makes others want to be like you

3. Association: who one knows, being in the right social groups, going to the right schools, marrying the right people

Employees with a certain amount of personal power must be careful not to abuse it. Never underestimate your power — no matter how insignificant your position. Using the power you have to help your boss and the organization shows your boss you understand the value of teamwork. Review the "power" list above and ask yourself the following questions.

1. What kind of power do I possess?

2. Could I use it more effectively?

3. What kind of power do I need that I don't have?

4. Can I ask my boss to help me get it?

The key to using your power as an employee is to do the best job you can in your present position. Employees who make no secret of their boredom with their middle management boss, believing their destiny lies in the boardroom, will be left in the dust by more dedicated peers whose bosses have found them reliable and eager.

Directions: The following questions will help you know the kind of power you and your boss have.

1. How does your boss use her power with you?

2. How does your boss use her power with her boss?

3. How could you help your boss use her power more effectively?

4. How do you use your power with your boss?

5. How do you use your power with your subordinates?

6. What kind of power do you need to be more effective?

7. How can your boss help you have more power?

Reflections

Summary

The power pyramid is the basis of corporate structure — built on the dual concepts of rank and chain of command. Your boss's position carries certain powers. Your position carries certain powers. Your relationship with your boss is strengthened when you're proactive rather than reactive.

Your boss can wield two kinds of power:

The power of the position

Power to reward

Power to punish

Authority inherent in the position

Personal power

Expertise

Referent power

Power of association

You, too, can wield similar types of power — either positively or negatively — to make your boss look good or bad. Learn to play your position well. Being willing to work with your boss is the No. 1 rule. Power comes in managing the relationship.

3 ASSESSING YOURSELF

Before tackling the question of how to manage your boss, it's best to start closer to home and look at how you manage yourself. In either case, it's important to make a clear assessment of yourself, your skills and your emotional makeup. For those of you who already manage others or report to managers, it's also necessary to have a clear idea of what management is all about.

In this chapter we'll examine the following concepts: the art of management, managing yourself and assessing yourself.

The Art of Management

Management is based on describing objectives and measuring performance by bottom-line evaluations of profit and loss. Managing by objectives means working for measurable results, which can involve producing quarterly and/or annual profit-and-loss statements or developing interactive skills — helping others prioritize, communicate, innovate and become effective team players.

Managing well is more than a skill, it's an art — not easily mastered, but infinitely valuable to a corporation, an entrepreneurial group or a single individual. Good managers generate confidence in employees by demonstrating that they know how to take control of a particular situation, project or group of employees. They often teach others by the examples they set. Their validity and credibility as leaders become apparent in the way they manage themselves.

Employees watch their bosses to see how they deal with the four big testing grounds of a manager's mettle: how they set goals, how they deal with emotions, how they handle stress and how they manage time.

Managing Yourself

To learn how to manage yourself more effectively, start by reviewing your objectives. Once these are clear, it's easier to identify any problems you may have that interfere with managing your boss.

First, stop thinking of your work responsibilities as duties. That concept implies you're a passive worker waiting to be handed your next assignment. Show him you're an active, take-charge person. Start by thinking in terms of objectives, which aren't the same as duties. Objectives are goals that you need to assess over the short and long term. Once these objectives are clear, share them with your boss. Ask for his feedback. Make sure you both clearly see the direction in which you're headed. Once he knows you're serious about self-management, he'll be less likely to bother you with petty supervisory tactics.

Begin managing yourself by following these four steps:

Define Objectives, Measure Performance

Start by writing down your personal and work-related objectives in one column and how you will achieve these objectives in another column. Performance measurement should include short-term (daily or weekly) and long-term (monthly, annual) evaluations. Your page might look something like this:

Objective: Improve participation and productivity during staff meetings. Build a greater sense of team spirit.

Action: Communicate the purpose of meetings more clearly by providing detailed agendas. Seek feedback from participants and boss.

Monthly evaluation: Better attendance, more informed discussion during meeting.

Annual evaluation: Department morale higher, better team spirit.

Prioritize Responsibilities

Another effective management tool is learning how to prioritize. Managers rarely have responsibilities or projects that don't overlap.

Write down everything you do over a week's time, then take a look at tasks that are routine, yet time-consuming. If possible, delegate these tasks. Opening the mail, for instance, and tagging the important correspondence can usually be handled by a secretary or an assistant. Ask yourself how many of these duties could be accomplished by an employee, like returning less-important telephone calls, composing standard memos, proofreading documents done by word processing department or preparing conference room for meetings: supply clients with writing supplies, agendas, etc.

If delegating to an employee is not an option for you, try handling your mundane tasks in less time-consuming ways. You could combine tasks — open mail while returning phone calls or placing conference calls. Plan ahead: when preparing a conference room will interfere with other more important tasks, assemble supplies beforehand. Just say "no" — politely. If your boss asks you to interrupt important work to do a less important task, find a diplomatic way to make him see your priorities your way. Offer to do the other task later.

By prioritizing, your boss will get the picture that you have work under control. He'll be impressed by your professionalism. Learn to look at the big picture and decide what's really important for you to do for your boss. The higher your boss rises in the company, the more he'll be deluged with trivial paperwork. You can free up his energy to do what he's best at by keeping your eye on your targeted professional objectives.

By accomplishing these objectives in a proactive way, you'll not only position yourself favorably with your boss, you'll get a feeling for how *he* prioritizes *his* objectives. You might even be able to help him prioritize.

Be Flexible

Just as prioritizing is essential, it's also important to be flexible when changes occur. It may appear, at first glance, that your boss is incapable of making a decision and sticking to it. However, his actions could be determined by behind-the-scenes action you have no knowledge of. Deadlines are often delayed, and sometimes whole projects are abandoned while new ones are substituted.

Realize that it's the nature of things to change — especially in corporate America. Be able to accept new schedules, adjust your objectives and move forward actively. By accepting change you'll not only demonstrate your professionalism, but you'll make his job a lot easier.

Savvy employees take advantage of the opportunities available to them during change to move upward in their organization. Whether your company is undergoing a merger or your department is getting new office furniture, show that you're able to deal with delays and uncertainty. Don't rigidly cling to old game plans. Instead, make up new ones. Seize opportunities by being receptive to your boss's new strategies. Even with a boss who frequently changes his mind, don't throw in the towel. Throw your support behind the new game plan, have fun with it and plan to stick to it — until things change.

Becoming a Team Player, Building Trust

You may be on a team of one or 200, but being a team player is what counts. The ability to cooperate with others is the prime requirement for most jobs. It shows your fellow office workers that you're not playing the game to achieve your own ends but for the good of the team. How can you build better team skills?

First of all make sure that group goals and objectives are clearly defined and communicated. A corporate team is not much different from a sports team. You might even find that your boss has used some of the following football strategies in corporate team-building: perceive the goal, devise a strategy on how to reach it, motivate the team to do it and prepare to counteract attempts to prevent it.

Keep in mind that one of your group's implicit goals is to forge better interpersonal relationships — a payoff of teamwork that builds mutual trust among employees and identification with the company. An important dynamic of interpersonal relationships is that the more an individual sublimates his individuality for the good of the team, the more his individuality is appreciated and acknowledged.

It's important for employees to know their bosses trust them to do their jobs without being overly supervised. Persuade your boss to assign open-ended tasks. He'll be relieved of extra work, and he'll simultaneously demonstrate his confidence in your ability to act independently.

Trust fosters better relationships both up and down the corporate ladder in the following ways. It encourages a better flow of information, allows greater creativity and promotes acceptance of individuals for who they are.

A good manager's job is very similar to a good coach's. A boss who is able to coach knows how much supervision employees require. And once a player knows the goal and game plan, a coach's job is to let go. If your boss is a good coach, he'll let you carry the ball and win the game. Show your boss you trust him to let you do a good job. And then do it.

21

Assessing Yourself

Assessing your strengths, weaknesses, skills and strategies is one of the most difficult but productive exercises you can undertake to become a more effective manager of your boss. Having an objective understanding of who you are allows you to accept the parts you like and work on changing the ones you don't. It also makes it easier to separate your boss's constructive feedback from his unwarranted criticism.

What are your goals?

Companies have mission statements; so should you. Take time to write down both long- and short-term goals. Start with the short-term goals because they will feed into long-term goals. Be as creative as you like. Don't limit yourself by defining goals that can be achieved only at your present job. Long-term goals can relate to work, family, hobbies and recreation, any part of your life you want to seriously develop.

Now, prioritize the list. As much fun as writing a romance novel would be, chances are it's going to be outranked by finishing the documentation project at work. Yet spending more time with your children and husband is clearly an important consideration. Better time management and constant reprioritizing and delegating small tasks could free up some time and energy to spend with the family.

Look for the fundamental issues: your commitment to your family; the need for advancement and recognition at work; a desire to take on a creative project; etc. It is important that you understand what issues are basic to your life and their priority. This understanding will help you resolve conflicts.

For instance, you are offered a promotion at work, but the new job requires a significant amount of travel. This means you would spend much less time with your children. What do you do? Do you accept or decline the job? The answer depends on the way you've structured your priorities. Here is a series of questions you can ask yourself to help resolve family/career conflicts:

1. What are my career goals? What are my goals for my family?

2. How have they changed in the past few years?

3. Do my actions interfere with progress toward realizing these goals?

4. What elements in my life are in conflict with my career goals?

5. Is the position I currently hold really the best one for me?

6. Am I afraid of failing to meet my goals?

7. Am I afraid of meeting my goals?

8. Am I prepared to adjust my career ambition?

These questions may prove difficult to answer, but you will feel more comfortable with your decision if you've clearly defined and prioritized the fundamental issues in your life.

Short-term goals are the steppingstones whereby you reach long-term goals. To achieve better communication with your boss and throughout the department, you could set up monthly short-term goals. For instance:

1. Establish a method for passing on information to my boss. Make sure he is passing on vital information to me that he has gotten from management. If necessary, remind him that good communication allows both of us to do our jobs better.

Directions: Answer the following questions by circling true or false. These questions will indicate where there is opportunity to improve yourself and help your boss improve as well.

1. My boss sets goals and follows through.   T   F

2. My boss handles stress very effectively.   T   F

3. My boss deals effectively with conflict.   T   F

4. My boss is a good time manager.   T   F

5. My boss holds informative meetings.   T   F

6. I think of my work responsibilities in terms of objectives rather than duties.   T   F

7. I make a habit of writing my objectives down as well as my plan for how I will achieve them.   T   F

8. I break down my objectives into sub-objectives and evaluate my performance against my long- and short-range plans.   T   F

9. I keep a prioritized list of things I'm responsible for.   T   F

10. I manage this "list" by delegating or combining tasks.   T   F

11. I am flexible at adjusting my priorities to my boss's.   T   F

12. I see my boss, myself and my peers in a team-coach relationship.   T   F

Reflections

2. When appropriate, schedule weekly meetings between staff and management to keep projects on schedule.

3. Solicit feedback from staff regarding the effectiveness of meetings. Ask for ways to help make their jobs easier. Is there training or technical information they need? Are the meetings helpful?

How do you fit in?

Consider your work habits. You may have just started in a new position, or perhaps you've been at your job so long you could do your work in your sleep. Has the grind gotten to you, or do you look at each day with its own set of challenges as uniquely different? Ask yourself the following questions. Am I dependable? Do I take pride in my work? Do I steer clear of destructive office politics? Do I try to learn from my mistakes? Do I approach problems as opportunities to learn new skills?

Dependability means being at work on time, sometimes arriving early and staying late. Your behavior sets an example to those both below and above you on the corporate ladder. Even a somewhat lazy and disorganized boss will improve his performance when he knows he has conscientious, talented employees on his team who are prepared for meetings.

Pride in your work sends another clear message to your boss and colleagues. Working by the project, not by the clock, means that if necessary, you're willing to dedicate time after work and on weekends to see that a project is done right and deadlines are met.

If you feel your dedication is eroding, find ways to counteract your sliding spirits. Find new approaches to doing your job. Ask for training on new technology. Job-share your present position with someone else in the company. Attend a motivational seminar. Find out how people in similar positions innovate in their jobs. Explore the possibility of using your knowledge and experience to train for a new job within the company.

Write your final mission statement here. Don't forget to prioritize your long- and short-term goals.

Now, read your completed mission statement and ask yourself where you stand now. Are you on track? If not, go back and review the "How do you fit in?" section.

Reflections

Above all, steer clear of harmful office politics, spreading malicious gossip and rumors. When you're in a managerial position, office rumors can be an important way of obtaining information you may otherwise be denied. But it's crucial to keep a professional attitude and to be supportive of fellow workers, especially your boss.

Summary

In this chapter we've examined some ways you can assess your own performance in the workplace. To better manage yourself, you've learned how to:

- Define your objectives.

- Prioritize those objectives by delegating unimportant tasks.

- Be a team player.

- Develop short- and long-term goals.

- Evaluate how you fit in with your work environment.

4 THREE OBSTACLES TO MANAGING YOUR BOSS

Emotions, time management and stress can seriously derail your efforts to effectively manage your boss. How you overcome them will have a lot to do with how effectively you interact not only with your boss but with co-workers and your employees.

Ask yourself the following questions. Do I become visibly irritated over poor planning and tight deadlines? Are relationships with my colleagues and boss complicated by unresolved issues in my life? (Insecurity, need for approval, conflicts with authority, for instance.) Do I have the resources to get the job done right? Am I constantly battling stress?

No matter how professional your demeanor or great your expertise, if you answered "yes" to any of the above questions, chances are you could be alienating your boss. Let's take a look at the three monsters that eat away at the most valuable resource any manager has: self-esteem.

Emotions

How many times has this happened to you? A male boss whom you respect highly suddenly loses all control one afternoon and pounds his fist on his desk, berating a trembling secretary. Or a female boss you admire for her ability to function under pressure is found sobbing over a minor addition to her workload. Even if you empathized with the boss, her loss of control probably made you see her in a new light.

Emotions can be volatile or chilling. They can make us explode with anger or droop from depression. No matter what their nature, the effect of emotions on our energy is draining. It's best to know what kinds of emotions you experience on a daily basis.

See if any of the following statements describe you. I hide or suppress my annoyance with others. I am frequently bored. I can't concentrate on my work. I feel pressured from all directions. I avoid involving others in decision-making and planning. When I become openly angry, I feel guilty afterward. I frequently worry about trivial matters.

If you answered "yes" to any of the previous questions, you may have problems handling one or more of these six basic emotions:

- Anger
- Joy
- Fear

- Depression
- Trust
- Anxiety

Everyone feels these emotions with some degree of intensity. They're a problem only when they keep us from performing our jobs.

Anger and depression

Some emotions funnel naturally into others. Unexpressed anger can lead to depression; unexamined fear can result in a heightened level of anxiety. Your performance at work will improve when you're aware of your feelings and know how to deal with them.

Surprisingly, feelings are often controlled by thoughts. Negative thoughts lead to depression, just as fearful thoughts lower self-esteem. Learning to monitor your negative thoughts is the first step to getting control of your emotions.

If you were to ask most people if they are angry, they would probably deny it. But here are some symptoms of unacknowledged anger: tense, tight muscles, speaking in a loud voice, knot in stomach, nervous mannerisms, quick, shallow breathing or increased heart rate.

People can suppress anger and bottle it up or express it in uncontrolled outbursts; but either way, anger is a particularly potent emotion. Unexpressed or poorly expressed anger can damage your relationship with your boss and fellow employees because they will sense your latent hostility and feel defensive.

Your feelings of anger, particularly with your boss, might be justified. Perhaps you have a boss who likes to deliberately upset and frustrate employees. Take your "emotional temperature," and see if you have any unresolved feelings of anger toward your boss. Try to be objective, and determine if they're justified. If so, clearly point out to her what it is she's doing that causes your angry reactions and explore possibilities for change.

If she's not willing to change her behavior, you should devise ways to monitor your own reactions before they reach the boiling point. You can excuse yourself for a "cooling off" period when discussions become heated. You can stay in touch with your feelings and give your boss feedback: "It's difficult for me to follow your instructions when you yell."

If your angry feelings toward your boss seem unjustified or out of proportion, chances are you're dealing with unresolved issues of anger from your childhood. Find out if your anger is chronic. Ask yourself: Do I lose my temper easily over unimportant trivialities? Does my boss's behavior remind me of the parent with whom I'm really angry? Is my anger predictable: e.g., certain times of the day (after breakfast, after lunch) when blood sugar is low?

Find a professional who can help you deal with your anger. It could be getting in the way of your career. When your boss sees you as overly emotional and edgy, she'll hesitate to trust you with important assignments. As much as she values your strengths and abilities, your volatile, unpredictable reactions might make you an undependable team player.

Depression is a feeling of sadness or grief. It can spring from unexpressed anger or stem from a particular event such as a death in the family or a failure at work.

Depression has few, if any, positive effects. It does tell you something is wrong. When you deny depression, preferring not to examine its cause, it can turn into chronic depression, which lowers your energy level and makes you unable to function.

The most effective way to cure depression is first to identify what's causing it. That can be relatively simple if you are suffering from an isolated case of depression caused by a major change in your life (moving, divorce, illness, etc.). However, if you are chronically depressed, identifying the source of your depression is more difficult. This type of depression can be driven by numerous complex emotions.

If you think you fall into this category of chronic depression, consider talking to a counselor, psychologist, minister or similar professional who can help you identify and correct the source of your depression.

You may have the world's most empathetic boss or you may not. But even a supportive boss gets tired of an employee who needs constant reenergizing to get the job done. Depression may cause you to feel like you're completely isolated; however, your energy level affects everyone with whom you work.

To work through your depression you may need extra sleep, more privacy and understanding friends. It's unlikely you'll find any of these at work. Make every effort to counter the effects of depression by getting to work on time, being decisive and taking pride in your work.

Avoid denying your depression by becoming a workaholic. Just do your job. Your boss will appreciate your professionalism.

Joy and trust

Joy is, or should be, a very real part of our daily lives whether we experience it at home or at the office. Joy restores our energies and regenerates our view of the world.

We've looked at what kind of power good bosses have. One of them is the power of personality, the ability to inspire others with enthusiastic leadership. Managers who lack joy are not inspirational. They can even infect employees with their own defeatism. By the same token, listless employees can make their boss's jobs much tougher if not impossible. The effects of joy in the workplace are limitless. It can motivate workers to participate in consuming, goal-oriented work, promote sharing, generosity and teamwork or allow workers to substitute the pleasures of discovery for the dull patterns of habit and routine.

How many times have we heard that it's important to find joy in our work? Your only joy in your dull job may come at five o'clock on Friday afternoon, when you're free of the office for a weekend. If this is the case, you need to evaluate what you're doing and see if you can find a way to improve your job or move on to something more fulfilling. If your outlook is decidedly joyless, it may mean your self-esteem is at an all-time low. Here are four ways to boost it:

1. Avoid comparing yourself with others. Your achievements and abilities are unique.

2. Reward yourself.

3. Accept praise and accent the positive. Don't dwell on past mistakes.

4. Avoid self-criticism.

Joy fuels you with added energy. It allows you to work hard, acting with confidence and decisiveness, pushing projects through to their final conclusion.

We've mentioned trust as a part of teamwork. Without trust, the corporate world would no longer exist. It's the glue that binds all relationships and agreements. Your trust in others can be limited by how much you trust yourself.

Self-trust gives you the following major advantages on the job. It allows you to recognize and rely on your abilities. It gives you confidence to cope with difficult situations. It provides you with the inner strength to act decisively and push for results that may lack popular support.

If you find yourself relying too much on the rules, unwilling to delegate tasks, suffering from disorganization or supervising your employees' work too closely, you need to improve your trust in others and in yourself.

Trust begets trust. The more confident and self-trusting you are, the more you will trust your boss to do her job. She, in turn, will recognize your support by showing her trust in *you*. Mutual trust among employees and employers allows you to bypass time-consuming red tape and cumbersome rules and regulations. Once trust is established, both you and your boss will be more innovative, and your jobs will be more fun.

Fear and anxiety

Fear is one of the most basic emotions known to man. It prompts the body to pump adrenaline in anticipation of the classic "fight or flight" situation. We experience fear almost daily, yet not many people would admit to being fearful. It simply doesn't go with the confident image demanded by the corporate world; yet we're all afraid of making mistakes, of displeasing our bosses, of losing our jobs.

Some people are afraid of not "fitting in," of how business associates would regard them if they acted slightly different or if their true natures were known. Some of those who have made it to top-level management jobs suffer from the imposter syndrome — they have constructed a professional "persona" that conforms to others' expectations.

A person in this situation may feel she has to be tough with her employees to appear strong, or she may become a workaholic and forego spending time with her family to conform to a hard-driving executive image. Unfortunately, these people often think: "This is not the true me. Somehow this all happened by accident." When fear goes unexamined it can produce a high level of anxiety. Keep in mind it is an emotion that won't simply "go away." To deal with fear effectively, you must recognize it and then control it to your advantage.

When fear is out of control, it can limit your social and business life, and it can prevent you from functioning effectively.

Ask yourself the following questions. Is fear limiting me in any way? Do I frequently feel fearful? Has my fear acted as a self-fulfilling prophecy on several occasions? If so, how?

Some fears are groundless, some are not. If you're afraid of displeasing your boss, try to ascertain if you're acting out of insecurity or if you have some reasonable motive. Perhaps your boss became openly hostile and punitive to other employees who displeased her in the past.

To overcome fear, it helps to rationally identify what you are afraid of, then think of a "worst case" scenario. Make a realistic evaluation of what is liable to happen.

Believe it or not, fear has positive uses in the business environment. It all depends on intensity and duration. Moderate, occasional fear stimulates; tremendous fear paralyzes. People are most fearful when they're learning a new job or defending a present one. You can benefit from occasional fear in two ways. It allows you to learn and evaluate new situations quickly. It can stimulate you to develop effective countermeasures.

One way to conquer fear is through biofeedback techniques: learn to relax, visualize yourself in a positive situation and make positive affirmations. Nothing can do more damage to your work performance than being afraid of your boss. You have to ask yourself if your fear is justified or misplaced. Does your boss bully and threaten employees, or does your insecurity with your boss's ego make you uneasy?

Some bosses like throwing employees off-center by behaving inconsistently, making unreasonable demands and alternately punishing or rewarding them at inappropriate times. Whatever your boss's behavior, ask yourself: Does she have anything to gain by making me afraid of her? What do I have to lose by being afraid of her?

Unless your boss is violent, vindictive or deviant, chances are she's testing to see how far you will let her go with her "obnoxious boss act." If you think your boss's bark is worse than her bite, try standing up to her. Fear of your boss is a major hurdle for you to overcome. Tell her how her behavior makes you feel and that you'd prefer she monitors it when you're around. She might not change, but she'll respect you for having the nerve to confront her. If, however, her bite is worse than her bark, you've got a tough boss to handle.

Anxiety produces feelings of uneasiness and apprehension. Anxiety can result when you are worrying about a future event rather than confronting a present danger. Many people experience anxiety in the following stress-related situations:

1. Time pressures to work more quickly

2. Evaluation of your work by an employer

3. Increasing demands or complexity of your job

4. Learning new skills

5. Health problems

6. Inner conflicts between personal values and job responsibilities

7. Coming into contact with a large number and/or variety of people

8. Getting a new job or a new boss

People experience anxiety when they have to make changes. However, many times these changes are positive. Anxiety can have positive effects in the workplace. It can, for instance, motivate you to attack a problem directly, help you analyze a situation and prompt you to set goals, reevaluate your talents and abilities, etc. In addition, you may have to learn a few more skills in order to decrease your anxiety level, such as becoming more assertive or learning relaxation techniques.

No boss likes to work with a worrywart. If your boss perceives you as being overly concerned with petty details or taking up her time whining and complaining, her trust in you will erode.

When your anxiety is justified due to unconfirmed rumors or the company's poor financial performance, ask your boss to verify the information you have. She may not be in a position to confirm or deny the bad news, but she'll appreciate you letting her in on the grapevine.

Emotional rescue

To get a better grip on your emotions, it's helpful to keep an "emotion diary." Write down what you felt each day, at what time and, if possible, what event, individual or circumstance triggered the emotion. Some emotions, like irritability and depression, are triggered by varying levels in blood sugar occurring just before or after meals.

Notice if a pattern starts to emerge. See if you're easily upset by the success of others, in which case your self-esteem may need bolstering. Check to make sure that the constant headaches, fatigue, colds and flu you're battling really aren't symptoms of depression.

Don't try to wrestle with these emotions on your own. If you're not pulling out of a depression or you can't get control of your anger, it's likely the problem goes back to subconscious patterns learned early in your life. Don't hesitate to seek counseling. When in doubt, go to an expert.

Time Management

The second obstacle you may face is time management. When five o'clock comes, have you completed most of the day's objectives, or do you stare at the clock, wondering where the time went?

Managing time effectively is one of the most valued skills you can possess. When you know how to structure your time, you show your boss you're organized and efficient. You also show her that you value time — both yours and hers — and that, as a precious resource, you won't waste it.

If organizing your time is a problem, ask yourself these questions:

- Do I get projects done on time, or are they continually late?

- Do I need to spend more than 40 hours a week in the office?

- Am I willing to forego breaks and lunches to meet a deadline?

- Is my work constantly interrupted by my boss, other colleagues, phone calls?

- Is there time at work I spend in personal conversation that could be limited?

- Does my boss dump extra work on me? Does she frivolously reassign projects and deadlines to suit her changing schedule?

- Is my style of time management compatible with my boss's style?

Time-management strategies

The way you manage time says a lot about the way you manage other aspects of your life. Do you arrive at work about 10 minutes late, wander into the lunch room for coffee and catch up on the morning's gossip with co-workers? Or do you arrive a little early, directed and focused, with a list of what you plan to accomplish? Now ask yourself, if you were the boss, which kind of employee would you prefer working with?

Maybe you'd like to be more like the employee in the second scenario, but getting organized is a problem. Once you're seated at your desk, phones start ringing, people drop by to visit and the day has taken off in a direction all its own. Priorities take the form of crisis management.

One way of gaining control of your time is to make a "To Do" list either before or as soon as you arrive at work. Include high, medium and low priorities. Work on one project at a time. Don't begin several projects at once. Don't take on extra projects until everything on the "To Do" list is finished.

To avoid interruptions while working on your "To Do" list, try some of the following strategies. If you have an office door, shut it. Ask the people at the switchboard to hold your calls or put your phone on "do not disturb." When co-workers drop by to chat, explain you're busy and then set up a time when you can get back to them.

Time management and your boss

You and your boss's ideas of time management may be diametrically opposed. Perhaps you're highly organized, and your boss prefers to work more intuitively. Styles don't matter as long as both of you manage to get your respective jobs done. What *does* matter is when your respective styles of time management interfere with one another's effectiveness.

Ask yourself if any of these scenarios fits your relationship with your boss:

Scenario #1:

Your boss is a stickler for meeting deadlines and commits 50 to 60 hours of her working week to the office. You, on the other hand, enjoy spending time with your family and have outside interests and lots of friends at work.

You think your boss:

- Is too hard-driving

- Should spend more time with her family

- Worries too much about job performance; she has her boss's support and can afford to relax more often

- Interferes too much with your work style; would like you to work from a "To Do" list every day

Your boss perceives you as:

- Spending too much time socializing at work

- Disorganized and unmotivated

- Lacking in company loyalty

- Not helping her meet her deadlines

Scenario #2:

Your working style is dedicated and effective, but your boss's style is laid back. While you like to pre-plan projects and meetings, she takes each day as it comes. You've already planned the vacation you're taking a year from now, but your boss may take next week off … she isn't sure yet.

You perceive your boss as:

- Relying on you to organize her

- Irresponsible and lazy

- Lacking an overall game plan for the department

- Standing in your way of possible advancement

Your boss sees you as:

- Too rigid and obsessive about time planning

- Wanting to control her

- Ambitious and easily frustrated

- Organized, yet overbearing

- Not well-liked by colleagues

In both scenarios, differing attitudes about time management can lead to real conflict between employee and boss. You may be better organized than your boss, especially if your boss depends on personal power to strengthen her position. Some bosses expect their employees to be better time managers than they are. Learn how to offer your time-management skills to your boss without alienating her. The overall goal is to build a strong team and become a better player.

Here are some time-management tips:

1. Construct a time log for the hours you spend at work. Include the time it takes you to dress and drive to work. Try keeping a diary at work that records time in 10-minute segments. Time at work can be allocated to three types of activities:

   - *Fixed activities* — staff meetings, production reviews, administrative matters

   - *Semi-flexible activities* — routine correspondence, meetings with customers, supervising employees

   - *Variable activities* — items beyond your control: phone calls, visits, personal matters handled during work hours

2. Once you know how your time at work is spent, compare it with your short-term goals for the day and for the week. Recognize the link between activities and goals. Each time you undertake an activity, ask yourself the following questions. Is this activity leading me toward or diverting me from a larger goal? Is it possible to combine activities so that I can free up bigger blocks of time?

Stress

Stress is part of daily life, and it can become a serious obstacle. Driving in heavy traffic can produce stress; so can winning a marathon. Many Type A high achievers find pleasure in the slight buzz they experience from so much to do in so little time. It's important to remember that stress can be caused by too many problems or too much success. Either way, your body interprets it as an overload of stimuli and responds by telling the adrenals to kick into high gear.

Stress, when not handled properly, can quickly escalate through various stages, beginning with anxiety and ending in a total inability to function. At this last stage, stress is your body's way of "just saying no" — and it means it. Stress in the workplace often occurs when you take on too much. You feel it's your job to solve not only your own problems but those of your boss and staff as well. Yet despite an overloaded schedule, overwork will not kill you. Recent studies indicate that stress can limit your life expectancy only when you don't experience enough joy in your accomplishments.

Look at what you do. Evaluate how stressful your job is. Think about the issues involved in the discussions on emotions and time management. Unresolved emotional conflicts or poor time management can also add to your level of stress.

Keep in mind that the group with the highest level of stress in America is not overly committed CEOs or hard-driven entrepreneurs ... it is clerical workers. The reason? They have very little control over their working lives. At the bottom of the corporate ladder, they are subject to the whims of various bosses, personnel departments and warring corporate factions in need of their services.

To assess the built-in stress of your position, ask yourself the following questions: Is my job stressful within itself (e.g., high pressure to perform, to meet deadlines)? Do I make it more stressful than it needs to be? Does my boss make it more stressful than it needs to be? Do I have any personal power in this position? How many bosses must I please? Am I meeting overall goals in this position? How does stress affect my relationship with my boss?

Even if you and your boss see eye to eye, stress still affects your working relationship. See if any of these situations fit:

- Your boss loads you down with plenty to do, but after you've met tough deadlines, she fails to recognize your accomplishments.

- Your boss increases your responsibilities but doesn't give you the resources (position or staff) to accomplish them.

- Your boss explains that you need to manage time more effectively but then derails you in a series of lengthy, pointless meetings.

"Joyless" stress comes from feeling disenfranchised, powerless and burdened with tasks. The more you take control of your life and say "no" to a demanding or unenlightened boss, the more stress-free you'll feel. It will also make you better able to interact with your boss and those around you.

There's a bad kind of stress and a good kind. You and your boss may both be the kind of workaholics who bask in the glow of a demanding but rewarding working relationship. See if you two share any of the following kinds of "good" stress:

- Passion and enthusiasm for your work

- Being centered in the present, refusing to dwell on past successes or failures

- Mutual resourcefulness: drawing upon each other's ability to constructively and imaginatively accomplish goals and create solutions

- Personal power: your boss has the power to influence the environment. In turn, she empowers you

- Perseverance: a mutual commitment to innovation

- Optimism: you're both open to new options and share them as often as possible

- Goal-setting: you're both good at defining specific goals to be accomplished within specific time frames

After reading this chapter it should be clear how important how you deal with emotions and stress is to managing your boss. Circle where you think you are in the following situations:

I get irritated and visibly upset when faced with tight deadlines.

> 1   2   3   4   5
>
> Seldom   Frequently

I lose my temper easily over what later seems unimportant and trivial.

> 1   2   3   4   5
>
> Seldom   Frequently

I oversleep or get into work late.

> 1   2   3   4   5
>
> Seldom   Frequently

I feel I have very little, if any, control over my working life.

> 1   2   3   4   5
>
> Seldom   Frequently

I feel my boss makes my job overly stressful.

> 1   2   3   4   5
>
> Seldom   Frequently

Reflections

Learning to effectively manage your emotions, time and stress is the first step in effectively managing your boss. It shows your boss you mean business and can control stress without letting it control you.

Summary

In this chapter we've looked at possible obstacles to achieving your goal of managing your boss: emotions, time management and stress.

> **Emotions.** We identified six key emotions and how you can deal with them: anger, depression, joy, trust, fear, anxiety.

> **Time Management.** Becoming a better manager of your time shows your boss you're organized and efficient. You can implement various strategies to help gain control of your time:

> • Keep a "To Do" list with high, medium and low priorities.

> • Avoid interruptions: phone and personal.

Assess how you and your boss react to the concept of time management. Are your working styles the same or different? Keep logs of how time is spent at work. Start linking activities to goals. Divide time into three kinds of activities: fixed, semi-flexible and variable.

> **Stress.** Stress is how your body responds to too many stimuli. Its sources can be pleasant or unpleasant events, all signifying change of some sort.

See how you and your boss create stress for one another. Is it "good" or "bad" stress? Is some of it avoidable through better planning or better communication?

5 GET SMART — GET TO KNOW YOUR BOSS

Knowing yourself is half the battle of managing your boss. Knowing your boss is the other half.

Hardly anybody really likes having a boss. In many cases the relationship all too closely mirrors the kind of relationship we had with our parents. Bosses tell us what to do, criticize our work, prioritize our tasks and time and ultimately decide our future with the company. It's easy to fall into the trap of responding to our bosses the way we did to our parents: like overly compliant "good" kids or sullen, rebellious teenagers. Neither kind of behavior earns us a boss's trust. No matter how gruff or intimidating a boss may be, the last thing he needs is an apple polisher or a terrorist.

A good boss welcomes strong employees who aren't afraid to tell him when a problem exists. How that relationship develops is mostly up to you. The first step in managing your boss is to realize your boss is fallible, a human being just like you, with measurable strengths and weaknesses.

To get to know your boss better, assess the following:

- His goals

- His power

- His particular strengths and skills

- How he handles his emotions and those of others

- His personal style

- How he handles stress

- His needs

- What he's like outside the office

What Are My Boss's Goals?

You spent some time in Chapter 3 defining and prioritizing your goals and objectives. What if you could take a look at a similar list of your boss's goals? It would tell you a lot about the person you're working for.

Ask your boss if he's willing to share a list of work-related goals and strategies with you — both short-term and long-term. He may not even have defined them for himself. Or he may prefer to rely on a less structured approach — by verbalizing goals in project meetings.

Even if your boss is reticent about communicating his goals, you probably are familiar with some of them from your day-to-day contact. List the projects he is in charge of; also think about where he wants to go in the corporate structure. Then make a list of his goals. Include what you perceive are his commitments to family, religious community and favorite recreations. Don't worry about putting them in any particular order. It's more important to rely on your intuition and spontaneity in this exercise. Your list might look something like this:

My boss's goals

1. Get marketing project in on time and under budget.

2. Become a better golfer, or at least find a way to deal with frustration.

3. Keep his boss satisfied and off his back.

4. Spend more time with kids and coach his son in baseball.

5. Arrange to spend more time with his wife.

6. Develop a modified projection of sales for the next quarter based on sales figures from branches.

7. Successfully present the new quarterly projection to his boss.

8. Help start a Neighborhood Watch group.

9. Be under consideration for the Marketing Director position.

When Your Boss's Goals Are in Conflict

One common source of boss-employee friction is when your boss has goals that conflict with one another. If appropriate, check out the above list with your boss. Be tactful and diplomatic, and limit your discussion to business goals. (He probably won't be comfortable discussing personal and family goals with you.) By reviewing the list and using your intuition and observations regarding his personal and family goals, you'll be able to spot the problem areas. What kind of additional responsibilities does your boss have? Is he willing to make further sacrifices of time and energy with two small children at home?

What Kind of Power Does My Boss Have?

Review the power pyramid in Chapter 2 and see where your boss fits in. Ask yourself what kind of access he has to the following resources: increased budget for staff or supplies, time to devote to company planning and powerful allies in high places.

Getting a clear picture of what kind of resources your boss actually has gives you a more practical understanding of what he can do for his employees. Now look at the six kinds of power outlined in Chapter 2. Evaluate what kind of power your boss brings to his relationship with you and to what degree.

The Power of the position

1. The power to reward

- Is your boss in a position to give you a promotion or a raise? If so, is it only during an annual review, or can he confer immediate raises and bonuses?

- How does he recognize you for a job well done?

  — *Informal recognition*: word of mouth, taking you out to lunch

  — *Formal recognition*: company newsletter, memo to others, including you in meetings and seminars

  — *Mentoring*: an acknowledged commitment on his part to take you under his wing to develop your promotability

2. The power to punish

- Does he have the power to fire you?

- Does he have the power to redefine your job responsibilities or transfer you to another department?

- Does he have the capability of undermining you so you'll quit? For example:

— *Subverting* your authority over your employees

— *Undermining* your support from other bosses within the company

— *Damaging* your credibility by assigning you dead-end or problem projects

3. *Authority*

- Does his authority come with the position?

- How effectively does he use it? Is he:

— Authority*philic?* Does he love exerting authority and overrunning his bounds?

— Authority*phobic*? Is he afraid to claim it; does he run the risk of losing it?

Personal power

1. *Expertise*

- Is your boss an expert at a particular function: marketing strategy, computer programming, architectural engineering?

- Does he share his knowledge readily with others?

- Is he grooming someone to take his place?

- Does he expect you to easily grasp what only he understands?

- Is he willing to teach you?

2. Referent power

- Does he possess a tremendous amount of charm, charisma and integrity that makes others want to be like him?

- Is he well-known and well-liked throughout the company, community and city?

- Does he rely solely on charm to get others to do his job?

- How does he interact with friends and family? In the same manner or differently?

- Can his connections help you get where you want to go?

3. Association

- Does your boss "come from the right family" or know the right people?

- Does his social background help or hinder him in doing his job well?

- Does he overlook your strengths because you're not from the same background?

- Did he marry the boss's daughter; is he the boss's son?

What Are My Boss's Strengths and Weaknesses?

Make an honest appraisal of your boss's strong and weak points. Maybe you've been so overwhelmed by his charismatic personality that you've never stopped to realize he's a little short on technical skill. Bosses, just like other people, need help in the areas where they're weakest. If your boss really knows how to motivate his staff but lacks ability to follow through, he may need some organizational help.

Start observing your boss in action, and keep a list of how he innovates, operates and motivates others — a kind of "report card" you can update regularly. Remember, the objective is not to indulge in excessive fault-finding but to see your boss in a new light, as a multifaceted human being. Ideally, you'll discover a way to lend your boss a hand, make him look better and forge a stronger working relationship.

Your evaluation could look something like this:

Perceived strengths

- Manages time efficiently

- Good listener

- Fair-minded

- Good technical background

- Has integrity

- Defends his employees

Perceived weaknesses

- Doesn't use all the resources available to the department

- Too detail-minded; loses sight of the big picture and long-range objectives

- Not perceived as a strong leader within the company

By comparing what you perceive to be your boss's strengths and weaknesses, you'll get a good feel for where he's effective and where he could use some help. The above individual has a lot of technical expertise and is a caring, loyal boss who goes to bat for his employees. He's not a charismatic or skillful enough corporate player to claim much of the company's resources, such as a bigger budget for more computer terminals, additional staff or raises. Chances are, his most ambitious employees will want to work for a more powerful supervisor in a department where the heavy-hitters are and where the stakes are higher.

It's important to realize that *your* attitude can enhance both your boss's strengths and his weaknesses. Remember, all bosses are judged by how well they perform for their immediate superiors *and* how well they motivate their employees. That's where you come in. Eventually, you'll learn how to help your boss improve his performance. But the best way to start is to show him you're on his side, that you're playing on his team — a team that will make you both winners.

My Boss, My Coach

If part of your childhood wasn't spent in the competitive world of Little League sports, there might be some confusion as to what being on a team is all about. Being a team player means the following. Your ultimate loyalty is to the team. You carry out your role or assignment as expected. You are willing to set aside your desires and wishes for the good of the team. Once you're in the game, the time for debate is over. All team members must play as a team.

Men, generally, understand the concepts of playing as a team more readily than women because they actually played on teams as children. Traditionally, games considered appropriate for little girls have been isolating and competitive, such as jump-rope, jacks and hopscotch. If you played a childhood game or sport as part of a team, you soon learned the essentials of play from a good coach. Winning and losing aren't as important as playing well. There's always the next game. Rules are important; they're what you play by. By playing, you're constantly improving. Teammates are bound together by a higher good that overcomes individual differences.

Maybe your boss is the greatest coach since Vince Lombardi. Or maybe he has never even worn a football helmet. What's important is your boss's ability to be a leader, to improve the performance of his employees and to inspire trust. To find out if your boss is a good coach, ask yourself the following questions:

1. Does my boss understand the game?

- Does he communicate goals well?

- Does he have an effective game plan?

- Is he flexible; can he change game plans when necessary?

55

- Is he fair — does he play by the same rules he expects us to play by?

2. Does my boss understand the team?

- Does he perceive and use each team member's strengths and talents?

- Does he trust us to win?

- Does he inspire us?

- Is he consistent?

- Does he empower us?

- Does he test our abilities by giving us difficult roles to play?

- Does he reward us?

And, finally, the most important question:

3. Does my boss make it fun to play on his team?

- Do team members enjoy playing on his team?

- Do others want to play on this team?

Being a good coach doesn't mean having all the answers. Good bosses solicit feedback from employees. It shows they respect their employees' opinions and trust them to be truthful. Evaluate how receptive your boss is to the two basic types of feedback: positive criticism and helpful suggestions.

- Can you openly discuss problems with your boss?

- How does he respond when you make suggestions?

— Thanking you for your concern

— Denying your feedback

— Defending himself

- Does he accept feedback only from his immediate superiors?

- How does he relay performance feedback to you?

— Directly, through meetings or performance reviews

— Indirectly, through other employees or departments

How my boss deals with emotions

Your boss's team-building ability can be affected by the way he handles his emotions. The facts of life apply at the office as well as at home: people are full of human frailties. Disguise it as they might behind tough façades or curt communication, bosses, like employees, have to deal with the emotions that arise as a result of failure. Evaluate your boss in the following areas:

- ***Keeping a positive mental attitude.*** Perhaps he failed once and is too afraid of failing again to really try.

- ***Separating the process from the product.*** If his strategies were good but the effort failed, it might not be his fault.

- ***Avoiding perfectionism.*** The workplace is full of distractions and conflicting priorities that call for compromise and doing the best job possible, then moving on. Don't dwell on how much better a project could have been.

- ***Learning to value failure.*** Growth and discovery can't take place without failure. Learn to live with it as a fact of life.

- ***Trusting and empowering employees.*** They're here to learn how to do their jobs. The better they are, the better the boss's entire department or product will be.

Depending on how well he deals with his emotions, your boss may fall into an "emotional type" — angry, effective or fearful. See if any of the following situations sound familiar.

The Angry Boss

Some bosses use anger as a means of controlling others — especially their employees. To this person, the advantages of bullying tactics far outweigh the disadvantages that may result from losing control.

Obviously, no one wants to bring an angry boss bad news. Inappropriate anger by a boss shuts down communication with employees and transforms employees from supportive to subversive overnight. When your boss is extremely frustrated, an angry outburst may be justified and can even be healthy. The key is: does he express anger appropriately and constructively? Does he play fair?

Ask yourself the following questions. Does he keep his remarks impersonal: focused on an action and not personal characteristics? Does he refer only to the situation at hand and not dwell on the past, reciting old infractions and mistakes? How does he react to an angry employee? Does he check his facts to make sure his anger is directed at the right person? Does he give someone a chance to explain before he gets angry? Does he make it clear *why* he's angry? Does he make threats? Does he provide alternatives or solutions? Does he chastise employees in private or in front of their co-workers?

Being the object of another person's wrath — especially when it's your boss — is upsetting and frightening. Try to stay objective and see if your boss has a valid reason to be upset.

List below your boss's four top goals.

1. _____
2. _____
3. _____
4. _____

What are three ways your boss uses his power of position?
1. _____
2. _____
3. _____

What are three ways your boss uses his personal power?
1. _____
2. _____
3. _____

List three perceived strengths and weaknesses your boss has.
1. _____
2. _____
3. _____

How is your boss like a coach?

_____
_____
_____
_____
_____
_____

Reflections

Some tough, overly aggressive bosses allow no room for error. If this is your boss's style (which is to say he treats everyone this way), it's important not to take his outburst personally. It helps to try and ascertain the underlying motive for his behavior, such as: He believes in the "drill sergeant" approach to motivating others. He has a strong need to control and intimidate others. He is a highly emotional person. In other words, his enthusiasm is as intense as his negativism. To see if you're reading your boss right, watch how he interacts with other employees and his superiors.

The Effective Boss

The effective boss has his emotions under control but is not afraid to display them when appropriate. He knows that without emotions, a corporate environment is dull and sterile. Emotions can be used positively to motivate employees, build empathy and foster team spirit.

Effective bosses are willing and able to coordinate plans, programs and people with intelligence and understanding. They let employees know where they stand and guide the department to meet its goals and get the job done within the limitations of budget, staff or policy decisions.

To find out if you are working for an effective boss, ask yourself these questions. Do his successes outnumber his mistakes? Does he handle failure realistically and move on to the next project with confidence? Does he avoid over-supervising his staff? Is he truly concerned with his employees' happiness? Does his department make money? Does he expect the same high-level performance from himself that he expects from his employees? Does he recognize and reward employees who have performed well?

Effective managers are good psychologists, using the varied emotional makeup of their employees to enhance their department. They know when to support employees who lack confidence, when to bend the rules for employees going through a difficult family crisis, when to give ambitious employees a chance to show what they can do. An effective boss prizes, above all, individual talents and abilities. He knows that a happy staff will require less direct supervision, allowing him to explore and develop his own strengths.

The Fearful Boss

Weak bosses often fear their own bosses and envy employees who appear more confident than themselves. A weak boss can sabotage you just as easily as an overly aggressive boss. Rather than ignoring weak and fearful bosses and hoping they just fade away, it's best to take the initiative and work with them. Try to find out why they're the way they are. Maybe they have just cause. Your slightly insecure boss could have been beaten down over the years by a bullying superior. Maybe all your boss lacks is confidence. You can help him become more emotionally secure by giving him positive feedback and encouragement.

Ask yourself if your boss has problems with any of the following:

- Working well with his immediate superior (fearful of not pleasing his boss)

- Working well with employees

- Not a good team manager

- Lacking in management training; promoted because of his expertise

- Handling a new position that has duties he is unfamiliar with

- Learning from past mistakes and not dwelling on them

- Willing to take risks

A fearful boss may want to minimize conflict at any cost, not realizing that incompetence can undermine employees as quickly as bullying tactics. Establishing the proper balance with your boss between aggressiveness and productive interaction is of importance to employees and superiors alike.

What Is My Boss's Personal Style?

Your boss's personal style can say more about him than his list of goals. His style, after all, is the way your boss wants the rest of the world to perceive him. First, look at his style of communication. Is he formal or casual, preferring written memos to verbal messages, or the reverse? A "paper person" likes to have information communicated first in readable form, followed by a personal talk. "People persons" are just the opposite — relying on meetings followed by detailed written reports. It's important to understand that your boss's style of communication is based on how he processes information. So if your boss is paper-oriented, send him a memo, even if you hate adding to the departmental paper chase. And if he's people-oriented, don't hesitate to set up a short meeting to discuss new information.

Styles of Management

Your boss's management style may be the product of a self-image that thrives on flamboyance and fun. Does he see himself as an adventurer, charting the unknown seas of corporate enterprise? Does he give free rein to his imagination in tackling problems? Chances are, if he's innovative and gifted, he allows his employees the same kind of creative leeway. If this is the case, you couldn't ask for a better boss. A daring and original leader, if allowed plenty of developmental latitude within the company, will recognize your inner resources and know how to make use of them.

A boss's style can often be shaped by his profession. Bosses who have served in the military or worked in law firms or government bureaucracies tend to be more formal, rigid and fond of doing things "by the book." A militaristic boss will emphasize the importance of the chain of command, reporting all matters to your immediate supervisor and following orders without undue questioning.

A boss's management style can change — particularly when he, as an entrepreneur, has more personal freedom of expression. When small companies undergo rapid financial growth, your boss's style may also undergo a change — from a freewheeling small business owner to a more corporately correct CEO, ready to interact with presidents of other successful businesses.

Preferred Lifestyles

Evaluate, if you can, what your boss is like outside the office. You could be in for a big surprise. The ogre that has everybody trembling before a staff meeting could transform himself into an adoring parent at the sight of his 2-year-old toddler.

It's always heartwarming to see a boss who's been cold and reserved at work exhibit warm feelings for his family and friends. You know that he has a life — a happy life — outside the office. The reasons for his hard-driven behavior at work become apparent. Your boss suddenly makes more sense to you in ways he never did before.

How your boss chooses to relax tells you about the other side of his personality. Differences in personality can be obliterated if you discover you and your boss share a common interest, volunteer for the same community group or belong to the same church. Suddenly, the boss you found so offensively loud and overbearing becomes more human. It's easier for employees to work for bosses who, like them, have commitments to family, outside interests and community groups that expand and enrich their lives.

What Are My Boss's Needs?

Every boss has certain basic requirements to sustain life within the corporate world. Bosses aren't omniscient or infallible. They need subordinates who will support them, keep them informed and, above all, intuitively understand their needs.

Some of your boss's needs are universal, and others are specific to your particular boss. Every boss, for instance, needs subordinates who can be counted upon for loyalty, dependability, relaying vital information, protecting the boss's time and sensitivity to pressures the boss is experiencing.

To truly understand the kind of pressure your boss is under, take a look at *his* boss. Is your boss's boss undemanding, fair and loyal? Does he willingly extend support to your boss for his projects? Or is he a tough, aggressive line manager who views each department's contributions in terms of profit and loss? Maybe there's a lot your boss would like to do for his employees but simply can't. He might be limited by budgetary considerations or a work style that differs widely from that of his own boss.

Companies undergo their greatest stress during periods of growth. So do bosses. If your company has recently undergone a merger, added new departments or changed its product line, try to evaluate what kind of pressure this creates for your boss. It's also stressful when companies shrink, cut middle managers' positions or get "lean and mean" for the long fight ahead. If possible, keep abreast of market trends and financial markets — any general economic factor that could have an impact, directly or indirectly, on your boss.

Once you've gauged the kind of pressure your boss deals with daily, you'll have a better feel for the ways in which you can meet his needs as a high-performing team player.

Develop Mutual Trust

Your boss needs to trust you just as you need to trust him. Being a trustworthy employee means being loyal to your boss and being dependable. He wants an employee who will support his decisions, avoid political games, show up for work and do the work.

Your trustworthiness is the solid foundation of your relationship with your boss. You may exhibit talent, brains and blind ambition, but if he feels he can't trust you, you're going nowhere within the organization.

Share Information

The kind of information you give your boss and the frequency with which you deliver it is up to your boss to specify. This kind of information sharing is usually done formally through meetings and memos.

But vital information doesn't always travel downward through the chain of command, nor is it always formal in nature. Sometimes employees are privy to information their bosses never hear. You can effectively sabotage your boss by not sharing this information with him just as you can strengthen his position by filling him in.

Information is channeled through informal conversations, the rumor mill and shared group activities: parties, the office cafeteria (or break room), bowling leagues, racquetball courts, country clubs, charity balls and bars. To separate what your boss needs to know from idle gossip, ask yourself:

- Is this information that affects his position?

- Is this information that affects the future of the company?

- Is this information something he needs to know about an employee, a project or budgeting that could affect his decision?

Avoid being a tattletale, spy or office snitch. If your boss hears you spreading destructive gossip about co-workers or other bosses, he'll assume, by process of deduction, that you gossip in the same manner about him.

Protect His Time

One of your boss's most valuable resources is his time. The higher a boss goes in the corporate structure, the more demands are made on his time. Since his effectiveness is measured by how well he accomplishes goals, it's up to you to help him plan his time carefully. Don't waste it in unnecessary conversations, meetings or phone calls. When reporting to your boss, make sure your information is correct, concise and not unnecessarily detailed.

Don't take advantage of his good nature. If your boss is someone who loves a good joke or indulges in mild banter, don't initiate such interactions when he's obviously pressured.

If you feel your boss could use some help organizing his own time, offer to help him with "To Do" lists, understanding priorities and turning time-consuming one-on-one meetings into more efficient group meetings. But offer only when he's not busy.

Give Him Respect

And finally, never underestimate your boss — even if you're convinced he's totally incompetent. You just might be wrong, and that would be a terrible mistake to make.

Even if you overestimate your boss's abilities, you've made the right move because you've gained an important ally. To get places within a company, almost everyone needs "help from above"; that means a boss who likes, trusts and respects you. And what better way to move up than with a boss who's going places? You might as well make the trip first-class for you both.

How does your boss express his anger?

_____

_____

_____

How do you interact with your boss when he is angry?

_____

_____

_____

How does your boss use emotions to foster team spirit?

_____

_____

_____

Is your boss a "people person" or a "paper person"?

_____

Is your boss's style of management rigid, doing things "by the book," or more flamboyant and "freewheeling"?

_____

What are some of your boss's outside personal interests?

_____

What kind of pressure is placed on your boss from his boss?

_____

How do you protect your boss's time?

_____

Reflections

Summary

Bosses are human beings, just like the rest of us. Show your boss that you are willing to take the time to find out what he's all about. Learn about his goals and how to spot when they're in conflict.

Your boss has certain kinds of power: the power of the position and personal power. How does he use them? Assess your boss's individual strengths and weaknesses, how he handles emotion, his perceived work style, personal interests and recreations.

Finally, find out what your boss's needs are. What kind of stress is he under? What does he need from you as an employee? Learn how to be trustworthy, protect his time and relay vital information. Observe the cardinal rule of all working relationships: never underestimate your boss. It's too expensive an error to make. By understanding your boss's needs, you'll see him in his full perspective — and you might even win an important ally.

6 MEETING YOUR BOSS'S NEEDS

Your one surefire ticket to increased job security, career advancement and graduating *magna cum laude* from the School of Boss Management is to know your boss's true needs and then to figure out how to satisfy them without, of course, compromising your own needs. In this chapter, we'll look at how to meet your boss's needs by:

- Doing your job and helping her do her job

- Evaluating her emotional needs and deciding when they're legitimate and when they're not

- Resolving conflicts between your needs and her needs

Many bosses, like the rest of us, have never actually identified what their needs are. They think of needs in terms of jobs awaiting completion, messy projects, piles of paperwork or salary increases and promotions. Your boss may need help with her job and not even know it. Maybe you're just the person to compile those dull monthly reports or add some sprightly prose to her upcoming speech. The trick lies in getting her to acknowledge where she needs help.

Meeting Your Boss's Work Needs

One of the most fundamental needs any boss has is the ability to rely on her employees to perform their jobs with competence and authority. This translates into your doing the following whenever possible:

- *Taking the initiative* — performing necessary tasks without being asked to do them, being a "self-starter"

- *Solving problems* — not appearing helpless when confronted with a problem

- *Using resources* — making use of the expertise or knowledge available in other departments (or outside your company) to get problems solved and work completed

- *Not complaining* — identifying problems and discussing them constructively when appropriate

- *Asking questions when you don't understand* — being organized when you seek help. Pick an appropriate time to talk to your boss; explain the problem concisely; list your alternatives, if any, and specifically explain the type of help you need

Remember, your boss is judged on how well *you* perform. Therefore competence heads the list of qualities you must possess to further your relationship with your boss.

Also, bosses expect their employees to display a level of professionalism that is comparable to their own. Demonstrate to your boss that when you are in the office you are there to work and get the job done in a professional, organized fashion. If your boss sees you as someone who behaves professionally, is punctual, thorough and dependable, then you will gain tremendous credibility and leverage — both of which are essential in effectively managing your boss.

Your Boss's Unmet Work Needs

Another area where you can meet your boss's needs is by helping her out with work that needs to be done yet isn't getting done. She doesn't have time for it, and it's technically not part of your normal work assignment. You can offer to help your boss out with some of her work, but be careful how you approach her. Depending on her level of self-confidence or how much she trusts you, your boss might interpret your action as an attempt to usurp her power.

Ask yourself if you can help your boss meet her work needs in any of the following ways:

When you have writing skills and she finds writing dull and demanding:

- Understand the core of what she wants to communicate, then write her longer memos and reports. She can then edit and give final approval.

- Ghostwrite her speeches.

- Proofread, edit and see that major bases are covered in interdepartmental communication she authors.

When you have organizational skills and she prefers to interact with people:

- Either put her on a schedule or ask her to share her schedule with you so you can make appointments when she's busy elsewhere. Confirm all appointments and changes with her at the end of the day.

- Introduce a new filing method or keep duplicate files of her work where you both have easy access to relevant projects.

- Convince her to restructure meetings so time is used more effectively. For instance, combine group meetings instead of holding numerous individual ones.

How effective you are in meeting your boss's needs is often determined by your approach. If she's open and enthusiastic and the two of you share a successful track record based on mutual trust and past accomplishments, you can be fairly open in your approach. Yet even the world's most confident boss doesn't like to be reminded of areas where she's weak.

Keep the following guidelines in mind when meeting with your boss to offer your help. Choose a time that's good for her — when she's not distracted, depressed by bad news or in the midst of planning for another meeting. Begin by complimenting her on something she does well. "Congratulations on the new contract you negotiated. No one else in this company could have handled it so well." Remain upbeat. Think of positive ways to express the help you're offering and why you're offering it. Stress the benefits you'll each receive. "I thought this would be good for both of us. Learning to prepare the monthly report would be a good learning experience for me and at the same time would free you to concentrate on more important projects that coincide with the report's monthly deadline."

Be open to her suggestions. If your boss agrees to turn over some of her work to you, she'll probably want to experiment on a project-by-project basis. Be discreet. Let your boss know you'll take on this extra assignment in confidence without advertising it to co-workers. Provide closure without pressure. If she agrees to think about your offer, close by giving her feedback and proposing a deadline for a decision: "We agree, then, that you'll let me know your decision by next Wednesday?" If she accepts your offer but doesn't provide structure, close by saying, "Then you'll get the report data to me by next Wednesday, and I'll give you a first draft by Friday?"

When your relationship with your boss is less open, you may have to approach her more subtly. When she sees that you're not only hardworking and dependable but also possess a particular skill that she lacks, she'll eventually find a way to ask you for help in the form of "offering you a chance to prove yourself." In this case, accept graciously and let her think it was her idea.

You can indirectly advertise your skills to help your boss with her work needs. Offer your services on a specific project to a lateral boss with similar needs as your boss. (But get your boss's approval first!) Ask your boss to send you to a seminar you want to take: on time management, business communications, etc. After a positive performance review, tell your boss you'd like more responsibility. Be specific. List what you can do. Can she think of a way to use your strengths?

And finally, be sure to distinguish between helping your boss meet her needs and becoming the unacknowledged "power behind the throne" who writes her speeches, prepares her annual reports and compiles the agendas for her meetings, all without adequate recognition or compensation. If your boss begins thinking of you as a blindly loyal subordinate to whom she can entrust more and more work without recognizing and rewarding you, then it's time to update your job description and insist on a performance review.

Meeting Your Boss's Emotional Needs

Some bosses need to know they're liked by employees. Others act like they couldn't care less. Maybe your boss is generous and fair but needs to see herself as a family matriarch rather than as a departmental manager. No matter what kind of a boss you have, you can help her be a better one by understanding her emotional needs and — when they're legitimate — meeting them.

Let's first identify some common emotional needs bosses have. See which ones fit your boss:

> ***1. Positive Feedback.*** Everyone needs to hear when they're doing a good job, even bosses. Your positive feedback can mean a lot to your boss when she's going through a difficult time. Single out one of her better qualities — her leadership, her fairness, her warmth — and let her know she's appreciated. Tell her you enjoy playing on her team.

2. ***Loyalty.*** You can show your loyalty to your boss by demonstrating good work habits, being punctual and focused and by carrying out orders without undue complaining or questioning. Reserve criticism of your boss for a one-on-one meeting with her. In turn, she should reward you by going to bat for you with upper-level management.

3. ***Respect.*** No matter how laid-back or fun-loving a boss you have, she still needs your respect. Your boss is never more vulnerable than in front of *her* boss or upper-level management. If you see that your boss has switched gears into a more structured, formal approach, do her a favor and follow suit. Don't persist in addressing her informally or casually dropping by her office.

By figuring out what your boss needs emotionally, you'll be fulfilling a subtle requirement that is never mentioned on a job description. When you meet your boss's emotional needs, she'll rely on you, trust you and confide in you more than she would a more highly skilled but less empathetic co-worker.

Unreasonable Emotional Needs

Occasionally, bosses make excessive emotional demands on their employees and co-workers. Their actions are prompted by unresolved emotional needs that seem to percolate through a bottomless pit of insecurity and low self-esteem. Ask yourself if your boss possesses any of the following characteristics:

1. ***Uses an Employee as an Emotional Crutch.*** This boss will use the intimacy that results from daily working relationships to establish an emotional dependency in which the employee becomes a substitute authority figure of the father/mother variety. At first, you may welcome what appears to be your boss's trust and confidence and eagerly respond with advice

or interested observations. Eventually, however, the boss's dependency interferes with the work that needs to be done, and you finally see that you are placed in a compromising relationship with your boss. Not only is it unprofessional, but it is emotionally draining as well. To back off may seem like career suicide, but to encourage such an exchange is equally harmful.

What You Can Do. Try to determine if your boss is going through a particularly difficult phase either in her career or at home. You might want to bear with her until the pressure eases off. If her behavior seems to be neurotic, however, don't think twice about ending your involvement. Chances are, if you create some distance, she will find another sympathetic ear. Set limits on your time and the kind of topics you're willing to discuss. If you need to discuss business with your boss and she wanders off the subject, listen politely, and then firmly bring her back to the subject. You can try nonverbal communication like looking at your watch, or simply say, "Did we reach a decision about how we're handling the sales reports?"

2. ***Overly Controlling.*** When your boss has to be involved in every decision, large or small, refuses to delegate and has trouble letting go of a project once it's near completion, she's exhibiting overly controlling behavior. No employee welcomes working with a boss who's continually peering over her shoulder, asking how it's going, substituting her way of doing things for your way. Workflow is interrupted, precious time is lost and employees are never given assignments through which they can prove themselves or better their skills. Oddly enough, what the overly controlling boss actually lacks is self-trust. Her refusal to delegate only mirrors her lack of trust in herself.

What You Can Do. When your overly controlling boss is interrupting you for the 10th time, tactfully tell her you'll be happy to incorporate any of her suggested changes once you've completed the project.

3. ***Not Open to Suggestions/Criticism.*** Your tough, intimidating boss may actually be hiding behind a façade designed to scare off employees who would offer her unwanted suggestions. Behind those intimidation tactics lurks someone whose low self-esteem will not accept criticism of any kind — no matter how kindly it is offered. Bosses who feel psychologically powerless often try to intimidate their employees in an attempt to exhibit their control.

What You Can Do. There are no quick and easy solutions to repairing another person's wilting self-esteem. Well-deserved compliments are likely to go unheeded, as are any other kinds of public recognition. You may experience a high degree of conflict with a boss who attempts to control through domination. No matter how angry you feel, try to remain in control of your reactions. Your overly intimidating boss isn't simply in search of a way to complete a task; she also wants a reaction. If you can give her the work she wants minus the reaction, she'll take her upsetting tactics elsewhere. Try to become aware of where her self-esteem is lacking. Then look at ways in which you can honestly bolster it without being obviously manipulative.

4. ***The "Moody" Boss.*** A boss who goes through several mood changes each hour isn't necessarily making unreasonable emotional demands on you. She's simply at the mercy of her own emotions and can't help displaying them at inappropriate times. If her spirits plummet from congeniality to black despair and back up again, keep in mind that her reactions aren't based on anything *you've* done.

What You Can Do. Rule No. 1: Don't take her reactions personally. Rule No. 2: Give her some feedback. Based on how open your relationship with your boss is, let her know how her psychological states affect clients, co-workers and upper management. It might be a behavior she's not aware of and can change. Possibly, it's something she can't change. When dealing with a "moody" boss, timing and anticipation are the keys. You may feel like you're constantly walking on eggshells with this boss, but the payoff is worth it.

When Your Needs and Your Boss's Needs Conflict

What happens when your boss's emotional needs infringe upon your sense of what's appropriate and inappropriate, right and wrong? When your boss's behavior goes beyond obnoxiousness and becomes psychologically dysfunctional, resulting in sexual harassment, dangerous threats and illegal practices, you need to act swiftly and firmly.

Conflicts with bosses often arise from different styles of working. Consider yourself lucky if your work style meshes smoothly with that of your boss. Here are some typical examples of conflicting work styles:

Employee Needs ...	Boss Needs ...
To work autonomously	To be constantly involved and continuously supervise employees' work
Spontaneous feedback/strokes	To remain aloof, protect her privacy. Views spontaneity as an informal style of management.
To have freedom to be creative	To control all aspects of work assignments

In each of the above examples, employee/boss needs differ radically. As an employee, you have management theory on your side that stipulates that bosses need to be responsive to their employees' needs. Here are some steps you can follow to ensure that mutual expectations are met without either party feeling unduly compromised:

- Evaluate how deeply ingrained your boss's work style is. How long has she held this position? Has she ever worked differently?

- Do other employees feel the same way you do? A boss may be more likely to listen to five employees instead of one about the need for change.

- Make sure you and your boss define mutual expectations. Be specific about what you need to work more productively.

- Be willing to compromise.

How can you use your strengths to make your boss's job less stressful?

_____

_____

_____

What tasks that your boss dislikes can you take the initiative to do or help with?

_____

_____

_____

What can you do that is outside your normal work assignment that would help your boss?

_____

_____

_____

What are some ways you can indirectly offer to help your boss?

_____

_____

_____

What are your boss's emotional needs that you can help with?

_____

_____

When your needs and your boss's needs conflict, how do you respond?

_____

_____

Reflections

Even if you're successful at negotiating only some small change in your boss's work style, say, initiating weekly staff meetings with an aloof boss, you've won a huge battle. It means your boss is willing to listen to what you have to say and make changes. Thank her for her cooperation, and build an impressive track record with her. That way, next time a conflict of work styles arises, she'll know that making a change is worth the trouble.

Summary

In this chapter we've examined how you can meet your boss's work and emotional needs. Your boss's main need is to have employees she can rely on to do their jobs with competence and authority.

Your boss may also need help with her own workload from a talented employee. A great many unmet needs among supervisory staff are tasks requiring organizational and communication skills.

Your boss also has emotional needs. Some examples of legitimate emotional needs are: loyalty, respect and positive feedback. You may also feel that your boss's needs border on the unreasonable, stemming from unresolved emotional problems. If this is so, see if there are ways you can interact with your boss to protect yourself and make her aware of the inappropriateness of her requests.

By meeting your boss's needs you can demonstrate your competence to do the job while building her trust in you to meet her emotional needs.

When you and your boss's needs are in conflict, it's best to resolve problems by soliciting feedback on mutual expectations. Be clear about the changes you need from your boss to do a better job; then, when she accommodates your request, work hard to prove both of you right.

7 BUILDING BETTER COMMUNICATION WITH YOUR BOSS

No matter how great a relationship you have with your boss, everyone can benefit from learning how to communicate more effectively, more efficiently and more clearly.

In this chapter we'll look at the following: communication habits you may want to break, how to communicate with your boss, nonverbal communication problems to watch for and how to communicate in writing.

Communication Habits You May Want to Break

The following scenarios illustrate some cardinal rules that pertain to the ways employees communicate with a boss. See if any of them sound familiar.

1. You tell all your friends what a great boss you have. It's almost like working for an older sister. You can pop into her office any time to ask her questions or just shoot the breeze. She often drops by your cubicle to tell you about her latest date, then inquires as she's ready to leave, "Hey, any problems with that last project I gave you?" Actually, you *do* have a few problems, but you hate to bring them up and ruin the great time the two of you are having.

2. You work for a guy you really respect. Everyone in the company agrees that he's not only good, he's brilliant at what he does. He's published articles. He's even been appointed by the mayor to serve on special committees. You realize this boss is on his way up. You've asked him for more responsibility, and he gives you a difficult project to accomplish within a tight deadline. You've tried a few times to get him to help you with some problems you are having, and he just brushes you off. You feel like you must be the most incompetent assistant he's ever had.

3. The woman who was newly hired to manage your department has never worked in sales before. Her background is in accounting. You can see she's making some very basic mistakes. In a staff meeting, when she asks for questions or suggestions, you offer a few helpful hints on how she could improve. Although she tries not to show it, you can tell she's irritated. She has ignored you for the past week now, and you don't know what you did wrong.

In the three examples above, the method of communication between boss and employee is not working to either person's advantage. The subordinate may not be able to pinpoint what's wrong, but he does sense that the boss is not giving him proper guidance to get the job done or that they aren't communicating well.

Example 1. What's going on

In the first example, the boss has encouraged her employee to think of her as a "pal." There is nothing wrong with a boss having an open-door policy, but when traffic is not controlled and employees rush in with fires to be put out, office gossip or questions they could have easily answered themselves, a manager's precious time vanishes. Likewise, a boss who drops by an employee's cubicle to discuss personal issues while ignoring the project at hand is acting irresponsibly and unprofessionally.

How the boss sees it

The boss can't figure out why her employee is so undermotivated and unable to meet deadlines — why productivity and work quality are poor. After all, the boss gives up precious time to listen to her staff whenever they want to talk.

How the employee sees it

The subordinate finally realizes that he cannot get his work done because of poor supervision and interrupted work habits. When the managerial axe falls, it will be on his head, not his boss's.

What to do

Both boss and employee are wasting each other's time in these chats. The employee should first change his behavior: greatly reduce the amount of time he initiates with his boss "popping into her office" and "shooting the breeze." If he is interrupted by his boss who begins talking about her personal life, the employee should suggest they postpone their conversation until lunch or chat after work. Finally, the employee must discuss any work-related problems he has with his boss as soon as they arise. If it becomes apparent the boss wants to cultivate a friendship, then the employee should suggest they get together outside of the office. Friends who work together need to be able to separate their professional relationship and their friendship.

Example 2. What's going on

In the second example, the boss is clearly not used to working within an office hierarchy or at least isn't skilled at managing employees. At first, the picture looked rosy to both the boss and the employee. They're both bright, ambitious people who value a certain degree of autonomy. However, when the boss gave the employee more responsibility, he obviously didn't pass along much training or helpful information.

How the boss sees it

The boss is used to dealing with people who have the experience to complete a project without help. The employee asked for a more interesting project, and he gave him one. Now he perceives the employee as a nuisance, always pestering him with trivial questions. With all his other responsibilities, he really doesn't have the time or inclination to nurse this kid along.

How the employee sees it

The deadline is closing in. If the project isn't done right, the employee will look twice as incompetent because he asked for additional work. The relationship with his boss seems to be disintegrating rapidly. He really needs help, and he doesn't even know how to talk to the guy anymore.

What to do

The employee needs to first clearly define the nature of the problem he faces and determine what it will take to solve it. Once the problem and the resources needed to complete the project are identified, the employee needs to determine if anyone else can help him. If so, he can seek help from others. If not, the employee should document the nature of the problem and the solution in a memo to his boss. The key is to communicate concisely. Most bosses hate having to answer a series of unrelated questions or deal with a problem in a piecemeal fashion. Then the subordinate should be assertive about getting a response. If he knows his boss is always in the office at 7:30 a.m. or on weekends, he should grab a few minutes of his boss's time then. If the employee finds his boss unresponsive, he should emphasize the importance of this project, his commitment to it and how he would hate for any problems to arise that could prove to be an embarrassment to either of them.

Example 3. What's going on

The employee sees ways to help his new department head be a better manager. He chooses the wrong way to communicate criticism of his manager — in a staff meeting. The relationship has been damaged by the employee's tactlessness and the boss's defensiveness.

How the boss sees it

The employee chose the most damaging time to offer suggestions on how to perform better. The boss concludes that either the employee is ignorant of office protocol or is consciously undermining her.

How the employee sees it

The employee believes he was honestly trying to help. Maybe the staff meeting wasn't the best place to offer advice.

What to do

The employee should ask for a few minutes of his boss's time to talk. At that time, the employee should apologize for embarrassing his boss in front of the staff. Additionally, he should acknowledge a lack of sensitivity and an appreciation for how his boss probably feels. He should indicate that even though they got off on the wrong foot, he wants to do whatever he can to support his boss. It is particularly important to understand that these two individuals won't be able to communicate effectively until the air has been cleared regarding the incident.

When communication breaks down, the fragile relationship between boss and employee can be irreparably damaged. The fault is rarely just one person's. As in marriages that falter, both partners in a working relationship contribute their share to the communication problem. If your boss is a good manager, he'll understand his responsibilities and take the initiative to put them into action. When the boss can't or won't attempt to solve a communication problem, however, it's in the employee's best interest to take charge and start looking for solutions.

Communicating Directly

One-on-one meetings with bosses are the most direct and focused type of communication. How well you conduct your meeting with your boss depends on how well you prepare.

Organize your thoughts. Know exactly what you want to talk about. Determine what the objective of the meeting is. Determine if your boss is a good candidate for a meeting. Choose the time and place wisely.

Defining your objectives and defining the problem are two different tactics. Before asking for a meeting with your boss, you need to clearly define the problem or issues you want to discuss. If your boss assimilates information better by reading, then prepare an outline or written summary.

When you are in the meeting, there are several things you'll want to do. Remain calm and objective. Describe the objective of your meeting concisely. Summarize key points that pertain to the topic of discussion. Present your conclusion, proposed solution or alternative actions that can be taken. Listen carefully to your boss's response. Does it indicate he understood what you said? If not, rephrase and summarize to correct any misconceptions. When responding to his concerns or objections, restate the specific concern; then explain your position. Seek common ground, points you both agree on. Seek solutions or an action plan that is mutually acceptable. Summarize any decisions that are made. Be sure they are understood by both of you.

Consider how you actually speak to your boss. Are you quick to put your thoughts into words, a little too glib, or does it take time to formulate your ideas? Hesitancy on your part can be construed as lack of job knowledge, whereas responding too quickly can make you seem impulsive or abrupt and rude. Practice the following:

1. Time your speech patterns by recording a conversation you might have with your boss. Do you need to slow down or speed up?

2. If you're having trouble verbalizing, give your boss some feedback: "Bear with me. I'm finding the best way to phrase this ... "

3. If you're too quick, give yourself some extra time to respond; count five beats before talking.

Think before you speak, and practice putting your thoughts into words. Sometimes we come out of meetings never having said what was really on our minds.

Not all bosses do well in meetings, especially when they're initiated by their employees. Defensive or angry bosses may try all sorts of postponing, stalling and interrupting tactics. Ask yourself the following questions to determine if a meeting with your boss is likely to be productive:

Can he take criticism?

A lot of bosses can dish it out, but they can't take it. Good bosses, though, want honest feedback from their employees. Realize that there are appropriate times and places to give your boss constructive criticism. The golden rule is never offer your boss criticism in front of others. No matter how well intentioned, it can demoralize and embarrass him; it can make you look tactless and blundering.

Is he a good problem solver?

No matter how buried he is in other projects, a good boss will jump right on a problem before it mushrooms into a colossal crisis. Ask yourself the following. Is he decisive? Not afraid to make a decision, even when it's wrong? Does he attack problems or hope they'll go away? Does he claim he lacks the authority to do anything about it?

Is he vindictive?

Does your boss seem open and accepting of what you're telling him, but the moment you're out of the office, is he sharpening his knives? If you're not sure of your boss's character in this regard, ask around. See if there were any co-workers who, after registering complaints or criticism, quit, were fired or transferred to other departments.

Is he honest and caring?

If your boss is honest, he won't betray what you've said in confidence to hurt others or hurt you. He won't use the intimacy of the meeting to lull you into a position of false trust, trying to get you to reveal things you may regret later. If your boss is caring, you'll know it.

Is he objective?

Can he see himself for who he really is? Can he see you in the same light?

One way to encourage a boss's objectivity is to be objective yourself. Your language should never be emotionally laden with phrases like, "You really screwed up when you..." Try to eliminate all judgmental words from your verbal communication. Words like "should," "ought," "good" and "bad" only inspire anger and defensiveness in listeners. Always make it clear you're communicating your *observations*, not absolute truth. Avoid sweeping generalizations such as, "Bill *always* makes mistakes." Stick to the facts. Back up your concerns with evidence.

Is he a good listener?

How well does your boss listen? You can tell a lot about his listening habits from nonverbal clues:

- Does he make eye contact with you?

- Does he nod in agreement?

- Does he ask thought-provoking questions?

- Does he reiterate main points when you've finished talking?

Or does he appear to be intensely uncomfortable, wishing he were anywhere but in the same room with you? A boss who is not listening will:

- Try to do two things at once: listen and read a memo, for example

- Play with objects on his desk

- Stare out the window

- Interrupt frequently

You might get your boss to be a better listener by suggesting you re-schedule the meeting or asking him for direct feedback on what you've said, thereby engaging him in the discussion.

Directions: Everyone's boss and work situation are different. Think of your boss and your work situation, and answer the following:

What are some of your boss's most dominant traits? (e.g., a good listener, doesn't take criticism, likes to solve problems, etc.)

1. _____
2. _____
3. _____

List some areas where your personality and your boss's personality clash.

1. _____
2. _____
3. _____

List three ways you would like to see your boss improve his communication with you.

1. _____
2. _____
3. _____

List three ways you could improve your communication with your boss.

1. _____
2. _____
3. _____

Reflections

Setting Up a Meeting

Following a few simple guidelines will help you achieve what you want from even the most indecisive bosses. You can propose the idea of a meeting to your boss either face-to-face or in written form, via a memo.

Tell your boss the purpose of the meeting. Don't keep it a big mystery. While your real objective may be to open up the lines of communication with your boss, this as a reason in itself can sound rather vague and imprecise. Have a tangible purpose and be as specific as possible.

If your boss starts waffling about a convenient time, don't take "later" for an answer. Keep confronting him (politely!) until he agrees to a definite date and time.

How to Prepare

If your purpose is to define mutual expectations, write a memo to give your boss before the meeting, detailing the problems you'd like clarification on. Stay specific. Avoid generalizations. Cite particular instances and dates: inability to get shipments to customers on time, problems in putting together sales reports, need for funding on a special project.

Remember, your boss doesn't have a lot of time to spend reading pages of intricately worded prose. If you've presented him with a 20-page memo *before* the meeting, he may lose all interest in accommodating your requests, foreseeing the mountains of paperwork you'll generate. Stick to the facts. Don't exaggerate. And keep an objective, non-accusatory tone.

How to Conduct a Meeting

During any introductory small talk and throughout the meeting, be aware of the body language each of you projects. It can tell you a lot more than the actual words the person is speaking.

Check for openness and genuine interest. Remember, this applies as much to you as to your boss. If you find yourself slouching in the chair, arms folded, turning away from him, sit up straight, place your feet on the floor and assume an attentive, responsive expression no matter how defensive his words make you feel.

Watch for body language with a positive meaning:

- Open, relaxed position, facing each other squarely

- Arms at sides or hands folded casually in lap

- Good eye contact

- Pleasant, attentive facial expression

- Good posture

If your boss exhibits some or all of these traits, it means you're coming through loud and clear, and he's receiving the information in a positive manner.

You should also watch for body language with a more negative interpretation:

- Crossed arms

- Body in a sideways position

- Frowning or stone-faced expression

- Frequently looking at watch

- Tapping toe

- Drumming fingers

If you see any of these traits, stop, unless your objective is to make your boss even more uncomfortable. One effective way of reducing negative body language is to engage your boss directly in the exchange of information. You can ask him for feedback by saying, "How do you feel about some of these problems I've touched on?" This way you can address any misunderstandings immediately.

Even when it's your boss's turn to do the talking, you still have to be watchful and aware, not only of what he's saying but the kind of information you're giving him nonverbally.

In stressful situations that carry an emotional impact, it's tempting to stop paying attention when the other party is speaking and think of what you're going to say next. By not "tracking" we lose part of what the other person is saying. It's easy for them to "read" our impatience to speak. Be sure when your boss is talking that you give him constant feedback, both verbal and nonverbal, by:

- Attending: assume straight posture, make eye contact, nod in agreement when appropriate

- Asking thought-provoking questions when he pauses for feedback

- Encouraging him by saying, "I'm really interested in hearing your reaction to this ..."

- Reiterating what he has said to let him know you understand

Asking thought-provoking questions may sound difficult, especially when you're already nervous about presenting your end of the discussion persuasively. But if you learn to listen closely, you'll pick up on key points. Asking your boss for further illumination will not displease him. In fact, he'll be impressed with your ability to quickly grasp his points of discussion.

Repeating what he said merely allows you to paraphrase his argument. You can begin by summarizing essential points: "You're saying that, first, we should eliminate undue spending within the department to increase production figures by next quarter. Second, that our re-staffing needs will have to wait."

Ending a meeting

A meeting usually ends with the two parties reaching a mutual agreement. When it's you and your boss, it's usually a performance agreement that satisfies the needs of both parties. Your meeting purpose and performance agreement could look like this:

Purpose of Meeting

For my boss to be more specific about what kind of informational feedback he needs from me and at what times.

Performance Agreement

My boss and I agree to meet once a week to discuss the written reports I turn in to him outlining the duties, accomplishments and status of my staff. At the end of each month, we will review goals for the next month.

Remember to make your performance agreement as specific and concise as possible. No one likes to leave a meeting with a performance agreement that is too imprecise for performance to be measured against. For instance, stay away from generalities like "schedule more meetings with boss."

When it's time for you to shake hands and come out of the office smiling, make sure you end the meeting in a spirit of cooperation. Thank your boss for his time. He *has* done you a favor, even if it's going to work to his benefit, too.

How to follow up a meeting

After your meeting, write your boss a memo detailing the important points and the decisions that were reached. You might want to include a phrase like, "If this is not your understanding of what transpired, please let me know." That way, should there be any future discussion of your not keeping up your end of the performance agreement, you have *your* understanding of the meeting's results in writing.

Arrange for a follow-up meeting in the near future to see how both you and your boss are dealing with the changes you've introduced. Remember, improving your communication with your boss doesn't come from a single meeting but from a series of fine tunings and adjustments until you have a system that works for both of you.

How to communicate in writing

As we mentioned earlier, all written communication, memos, reports and notes should be concise, well-organized and well-thought-out.

Remember the cardinal rules of memo writing. Never communicate through memos when you're angry. Never communicate through memos information you wouldn't want others to see.

Even when you write a memo that's "confidential and private," it doesn't guarantee that an unscrupulous boss won't use the information to further himself or to hurt you.

Realize that any time you write for business purposes, it's like advertising your own mental processes. This can work either for you or against you. Make sure your content is well-organized and structured correctly, ideas are communicated clearly and memos contain no grammar, spelling or punctuation errors.

Even though you may be able to blame clerical errors on your secretary, you're still ultimately responsible for anything that goes out with your name on it. Use memos and reports to communicate to others — including your boss — what a professional you are.

Directions: Keeping in mind what you've learned in this chapter *about your boss* — what are some potential roadblocks or pitfalls to:

Setting up a meeting with your boss?

_____
_____
_____
_____

Conducting a meeting with your boss?

_____
_____
_____
_____

Ending a meeting with your boss?

_____
_____
_____
_____

Arranging a follow-up meeting with your boss?

_____
_____
_____
_____

Reflections

Summary

In this chapter we've talked about how to build better communication with your boss through a series of steps.

1. Determine if you and your boss are having communication problems. Keep in mind that both boss and subordinate usually contribute to the problem. Assess the behavior and work habits of both you and your boss.

2. Decide if a one-on-one meeting with your boss is the most effective way to solve your communication problem. Determine whether your boss is a good candidate for a meeting. Prepare by clearly identifying your purpose, the projected outcome and what you want to communicate.

3. To set up a meeting with your boss, you need to ask him at an appropriate time and prepare a pre-meeting memo outlining what you plan to cover and the communication problems you're having.

4. During the meeting, pay attention to the nonverbal feedback you're getting from and giving to your boss. Stay focused and responsive.

5. After the meeting, be sure to thank your boss for his time. Follow up with any necessary documentation: summary memos or performance agreements.

8 BAD BOSSES: WHAT THEY CAN DO TO YOU AND HOW YOU CAN STOP THEM

Everyone — at one time or another — has probably worked for a bad boss. In some cases, how bad your boss is can be measured by how much she squelches your own career. If you have networked effectively within your company and have friends in high places, you might be able to tolerate your bad boss until you can transfer to a good boss. If, however, your boss is involved in unethical behavior or sexual harassment, you really can't afford to continue working for her.

In this chapter we'll look at some characteristics of bad, even intolerable bosses. We'll also talk about how they can hinder you by: blocking your career moves, taking credit for your achievements and undermining your credibility.

Then we'll look at some effective strategies you can adopt to deal with these individuals.

The Bad Bosses — Who Are They?

A recent survey of good and bad bosses showed that even good bosses are usually tainted with some bad habits or behaviors. It's not unusual for inspiring, charismatic bosses to display a certain amount of egotism or for technical geniuses to be a little aloof toward their staff. It all comes with the territory.

Incompetent bosses

If you work for a boss who's incompetent, chances are she's still got her job because *her* boss knows she's no threat and wants your boss exactly where she is. Incompetent bosses like to delay any kind of decisions as long as possible. Innovation is the bane of their existence; so is conflict.

To mask their incompetence, this kind of boss will form committees, set up fact-finding studies and hire outside consultants. But the real problems never get resolved, because incompetent bosses neither listen nor learn.

Incompetent bosses often have been promoted from areas within the company where they had some real technical expertise. They might have been more comfortable working as "independent contributors" than as team leaders; thus they tend to panic when management skills are required.

If you think you're working for an incompetent boss, compare notes with co-workers. Look for facts, not opinions or gossip. Find out, if you can, what her track record is with your company and with former companies where she has worked. Try to determine how soon, if at all, your incompetent boss will be led to the company's chopping block.

Executives often look bad if they promote or protect incompetent bosses. However, it might not be to your advantage to complain about your incompetent boss. Therefore, you may have to work with her, support her, organize her and do *her* job. By carefully documenting your work for your incompetent boss, you may be able to get yourself promoted and transferred into another department — something your present boss would never dream of doing for you.

Powerholics

The only issue "powerholic" bosses care about is that they're in the driver's seat. Working for powerholics can be a tough assignment. You've got to walk a fine line between being competent enough to make them look good yet not challenging them with your independence or ability.

The key word for powerholics is *control*. They've got to control every-one and everything around them, no matter how insignificant their place on the corporate pyramid.

Determine if your boss's power is real or imagined. Companies often give these individuals departments to control that have no real effect on bottom-line profit-and-loss margins. If your boss is merely a paper tiger, try to find out if there's a boss elsewhere in your company with some real power, influence and heart. Then make it clear you'd like to transfer to her department, where you'd be given more responsibility.

If your boss really does have power, find out if she's willing to give subordinates a hand-up by becoming a mentor. This approach may appeal sufficiently to her ego that she will help you. Whatever the outcome, look for ways you can learn from the experience — whether it is job skills you're learning or improved interpersonal-management skills.

Indifferent bosses

You'll know you're working for an indifferent boss when the workplace feels like a mortuary. Indifferent bosses cast a cloud of listlessness that is difficult for even the most eager subordinates to overcome. Perhaps their indifference stems from a woefully botched job of corporate casting. Their apathy shows; and unless you're careful, you could end up being just like your boss: indifferent.

Nothing is more deflating than being stuck with an indifferent boss. She usually holds on to her position through seniority or some quirk of expertise. If you complain about her attitude to other co-workers, they might sympathize, "But she's got to stay in charge of operations because she's the only one who can get this computer system back on line."

If she's burned out from too much job-related travel, family pressures or spending nearly every weekend at the office, encourage her to open up and look at some options, like a morale-building weekend retreat for the whole department, motivational seminars or weekly staff meetings to encourage feedback.

Remember, your boss's lack of caring permeates the entire department. Perhaps hiding beneath a shell of indifference is her way of protecting her job from ambitious subordinates.

Many employees find that the greatest joy comes not just from performing their jobs well but from the camaraderie that results from teamwork. When your boss denies you these benefits, it's difficult to keep the quality of your work high. In this case, you must evaluate how much longer you can afford to work for such a boss without your own attitude slipping. Assess how much energy you have, whether you can help rehabilitate your boss or whether you need to seek outside professional help.

Neurotic bosses

Nothing can make your job harder than working for a boss whose management style is impaired by her inability to control her emotions. This usually surfaces in a neurotic pattern of behavior that, depending on your boss's position on the corporate ladder, can affect the tone of the whole company.

Neurotic bosses have a million ways of keeping you in your place or helping you out the door. The last place they want to see you move is *above* them, *beside* them or working for another boss in the same company. They're afraid you're going to spill the beans about how incompetent, lazy, cynical and emotionally out of kilter they are. Good employees jeopardize a neurotic boss's security. Here are some ways to recognize a neurotic boss's style and what you can do about it.

Directions: Your boss may not display any of the bad habits or behaviors discussed in this chapter. However, it's important that you know how you would deal with these characteristics *within your own organization's* power pyramid.

What specific strategies would you use in dealing with the following bad-boss characteristics in your organization?

The incompetent boss

_____

_____

_____

The powerholic boss

_____

_____

_____

The indifferent boss

_____

_____

_____

The neurotic boss

_____

_____

_____

Reflections

Tough, Angry Bosses

You can be thankful that, as a trend, the "tough, angry management style" is almost over. But as a personality trait, a lot of bosses still believe it's OK to brutalize their employees in an effort to force peak performance out of them. The shrinking labor pool of the '90s has forced managers to put more emphasis on valuing employees rather than browbeating them.

What they can do to you

Tough bosses are usually valued by those above them, while those below them suffer. They manage to get the job done and to meet bottom-line requirements. Therefore, she's in an ideal position to do some real damage to her employees by discrediting them.

Undermine your credibility. As far as the company is concerned, your only window on the world is through your boss. If your boss doesn't like you or is secretly afraid of you, she can tarnish your record, deny your contribution and do her utmost to make sure no other boss in the company will welcome you into her department.

Block your career moves. The annual performance review is where it all happens. Watch for these favorite ploys of a tough, angry boss during your annual review:

The accusatory review. Tough, angry bosses do not like to reward employees, even hard-working ones. They derive power from throwing others off balance and keeping them guessing. Rather than recognize your achievements and contributions, your tough boss will berate you with your failures and shortcomings. Money is another big control issue with her, so she'll probably give you as little as possible.

What you can do

Tough, angry bosses are essentially bullies who enjoy intimidating employees. Their arrogance, however, does create a few blind spots. Your boss probably overestimates her control not only over her employees but with lateral bosses as well.

You need the chance to prove your worth to someone other than this tyrant. Look around. Surely not every boss in your company believes your boss is such a great gal.

See if there is a neutral party you can talk to: a company ombudsman, an employee assistance program. Make sure your job performance is good; keep records of your accomplishments, attendance and productivity. When the opportunity arises, seek a transfer within the company to a better boss.

Finally, stand up to your boss in an appropriate, self-confident manner when she is abusive or tries to intimidate you. If she makes accusations, insist that she back up her comments with facts. If she tries to intimidate you through implied or direct threats regarding your job security, tell her your work record will speak for itself and you'll be happy to discuss the matter before a review board or a mediating organization for unfair employment practices.

You can short-circuit the effects of the accusatory review by going into the meeting prepared with documentation of your achievements. Try to ensure that another boss is present. Bullies don't like to go public unless they're sure of their support. If your boss is allowed to prevail and you know she's being deliberately unfair, don't try to confront her. A tough, angry boss thrives on personal conflict and verbal abuse. Several courses of action are open to you. One is to go to your boss's boss. Another is to file a grievance.

When you go over your boss's head you've declared war, so be prepared for a vindictive response. Various schools of thought exist about when it's appropriate to go over your boss's head. They are:

1. *Never.* It violates the chain of command. Other bosses view it as insubordination.

2. *Sometimes.* But go only to lateral bosses, never to *her* boss.

3. *Situational.* When you have no alternative, go to her boss.

If you're going to complain to a higher authority, make sure you do it properly: make an appointment beforehand and have proper documentation. If possible, have tape recordings or notes in your boss's handwriting to refute any possible charges that you've manufactured the evidence against your boss. The purpose of going to your boss's boss or to a boss in another department is to hold your boss accountable, since she feels no need for accountability to employees.

If your boss's boss does not resolve the situation to your satisfaction, you're entitled to file a grievance. This procedure varies from company to company.

It sounds like it should work, but it often doesn't. Because of the office grapevine, the subject of grievance procedures, which should remain confidential, often doesn't. Depending on the amount of power they wield, bad bosses can escape unscathed, while the employees suffer the consequences of going back to work for the tough, angry boss they've ratted on.

You can also file grievance procedures outside the company that are handled through laws regarding equal opportunity and unfair labor practices.

Paternalistic/Maternalistic Bosses

Some bosses are most comfortable reliving patterns they learned as children, interacting with their mother and father. It seems logical to them, now that they're adults with responsibility for employees, that they assume the role of a parent.

There's the boss who views his subordinates as a "family." These paternalistic/maternalistic bosses may be well-intentioned, but they've overlooked the fact that the office is not the home. Their behavior is unprofessional and unflattering to boss and employee alike.

Paternalistic bosses, especially, are most comfortable assigning women stereotypical roles. They view female employees not only as daughters but wives and mothers as well. Female subordinates may find that paternalistic bosses refuse to take them seriously, preferring instead to patronize them. Similarly, male employees may have trouble deflecting numerous queries and advice about their private life by maternalistic bosses.

It could be that your paternalistic/maternalistic boss is trying to hang on to power by building a sense of loyalty through guilt. A boss often adopts this kind of behavior to mask a lack of expertise or competence. Be careful how you respond. Choose your remarks carefully. When confronted, a paternalistic/maternalistic boss can drop the parental act and turn mean and nasty.

What they can do to you

Basically, the worst thing a paternalistic/maternalistic boss can do to you is through power of association. Other bosses and co-workers in your company may think that you're just as unprofessional and ineffectual as your boss.

The paternalistic/maternalistic boss is often displaying a kind of passive/aggressive behavior. She excels at making *you* angry, however. And if you react negatively to her patronizing, snooping or cloying behavior, she'll merely respond with hurt bewilderment.

If you do too good a job working for Dad or Mom, they may be unwilling to promote you. Your department is just "one big happy family" as far as they're concerned, and you've found your place.

What you can do

When you meet with your boss, be sure to follow some basic guidelines. Otherwise, you'll get derailed:

1. Know what you want. Be specific.

2. Stay on the subject; reiterate your goals when the conversation goes off course.

3. Be professional. Don't make jokes, small talk or spend a lot of time listening to your boss's anecdotes. Your boss might see this as hostile behavior, but it's life in the real world — the world of business.

4. If your boss starts waffling, provide closure and structure. "A week from Thursday, then, I'm to have the improved sales figures for all my accounts to you for review?"

Competitive Bosses

Bosses compete with employees in all sorts of ways, both overtly and covertly. Men traditionally compete with each other, both as bosses of younger male employees and with their executive peers. Male employees are often plunged into fierce competition by top-performing female co-workers and bosses.

If you're a woman with a female boss, a certain amount of friction already exists. In a recent study, 47 percent of the women polled said they would prefer to work for a man, and 30 to 44 percent of the men polled said their boss's gender made no difference.

It's an acknowledged law of the workplace that women compete against women more fiercely and for far less reward than men compete against men. Even when you're a male employee of a competitive female boss, you're not exempt from her furious drive to prove herself. She may even see you as more of a threat than female employees because she believes you, as a man, are more promotable into her position. The best approach to dealing with a competitive boss is to find ways to promote teamwork with your boss and create a relationship built on trust rather than competition.

What they can do to you

Take credit for your achievements. Unless your achievements are documented and on file, your boss may try stealing your ideas and then stealing your credit and promotion. Competitive, unscrupulous bosses look for talented, inexperienced employees who will mistake their boss's sharpened interest in their new management strategy or a sales incentive as true appreciation.

What you can do

Employees will probably have to let the incident pass the first time it happens. If it looks like your boss is developing a pattern of taking credit for your achievements, you can:

1. Document to others your participation in projects, particularly to other bosses or your boss's boss if possible. Do this through: reports and memos written by you; active participation in meetings; working late/coming in early to work on a project and making sure other bosses see you and know what you're working on; suggesting an article be written in the employee newsletter (if appropriate) on your project; and saving any memos or correspondence that may support and document your role.

2. Push for visibility and recognition elsewhere. Realize that you may never get your boss to acknowledge your participation.

3. Meet with your boss privately when she blatantly refuses to recognize your involvement (not listing your name as the author of a report or participant in a project). Call the omission to her attention calmly and objectively. Ask for the error to be corrected.

Deviant Bosses

Deviant bosses look like everybody else. You can spot them only by working with them. And all too often, your career can't afford the damage they cause. If you suspect your boss of deviant behavior, it's essential you line up hard facts to support your allegations. Document your facts, talk to upper management and, if nothing changes, get away from her. As fast as you can. The following are two different types of deviant bosses.

The drug or alcohol abuser

Twenty years ago two martinis at lunch were part of a powerful boss's minimal daily requirement, just as low-cholesterol diets are today. Times have changed, and so has the public's awareness of the damage alcohol can cause to physical and emotional well-being. Alcohol abuse is easier to detect than drug abuse. If you see that your boss is openly abusing alcohol, chances are her productivity at work is slipping.

The symptoms of drug abuse are similar to alcohol abuse, yet drugs are deemed much less socially acceptable. For one thing, unless they're prescribed by a physician, they're illegal. Some upper-level managers have found themselves unwittingly trapped in a cycle of drug dependency that began as an effort to numb the stress they encountered in their corporate jobs.

What you can do

Many companies now have special programs for drug- or alcohol-dependent employees. Find out if your company has such a program. Find out who is the best, most receptive person to discuss this problem with.

Regardless, have your facts clearly documented. Present the information with compassion for your boss and from the standpoint that you're doing what's best for her and the company. Finally, request confidentiality. If your supporting evidence is convincing, there's no reason for you to become involved any further.

The sexual harasser

It's not unusual for conflicts to arise when men work for women or women work for men in the modern world of business. Although these conflicts may be job-related, they usually stem from underlying sexual tension.

Women bosses can sexually harass male employees, but the occurrences of such behavior are rare compared with the reverse: male bosses making female employees feel that granting them sexual favors is all part of the job.

Sexual harassment doesn't have to culminate in sex. It also includes any kind of innuendo, teasing, attention to one's dress, "accidental" fondling or pestering that the employee finds unwelcome and inappropriate. Bosses accused of sexual harassment often respond that the employee dressed in a provocative manner or was openly flirtatious. Therefore, it's imperative your dress and demeanor — even when "kidding around" — be completely professional and above board. Be prepared for lack of cooperation or denial when you ask your boss to stop. He may consider it all part of the game, that women say "no" when they really mean "yes." And if you go above his head, to *his* boss or register a formal complaint, be prepared for possible repercussions.

Some companies don't like employees who rock the boat — that includes standing up to a boss who sexually harasses female employees. Even if you have to leave the company to escape this situation, you'll know that by taking formal action against him — unlike others who silently and swiftly disappeared before — your complaint constitutes the beginning of a record against which your boss's subsequent behavior can be measured.

What a sexually harassing boss can do to you

Your deviant boss might use angry outbursts or physical threats to quell any thought of exposing his sexual harassment to higher authorities. He might use subtler methods of intimidation: threatening dismissal or tarnishing your reputation — letting it be known any attempt at seduction originated with you.

What you can do

If he seems unbalanced enough to carry out his threats or act on his anger, you should make your fears known to those who can restrain him. Document and, if possible, tape-record his outbursts, threats or innuendos; then take your case to the big bosses.

Public Strategies to Stop Bad Bosses

Confronting a boss is never easy. Confronting a bad boss is a lot harder because you have a pretty good idea, before you even start, how things will end. Most executives won't even listen to your complaints about your bad boss unless you have documented your complaint and confronted him first.

When an employee fails to stop a boss's serious wrongdoing by working within the company structure, she may choose to go public. Never go public without hard evidence that supports your complaint. The following are some strategies for going public.

1. *Whistle-blowing.*

Whistle-blowing means turning your boss in to the media, government agencies or law-enforcement officials. Employees who go to this length must be prepared to pay the price of a long and public fight. They're usually not still employed by the company they decide to blow the whistle on. Sometimes they're reinstated in their old jobs, but they're stuck with the stigma of being disloyal, demented, even dangerous.

When whistle blowers are still employed by their companies, federal laws now make it illegal for employers to retaliate.

2. *Legal action.*

For those disenfranchised employees who thirst not only for vindication but for justice, taking legal action against their former employers is now possible, thanks to the anti-discrimination and labor laws Congress has passed during the last 30 years. If you're planning to take legal action, find out more about:

- The Equal Pay Act of 1963

- The Civil Rights Act of 1964

- The Age Discrimination in Employment Act of 1967

- The Occupational Safety and Health Act of 1970

- The Federal Privacy Act of 1974

In dealing with the following *bad-boss types,* you often can be right and still "lose." It is important to know what's available to you from your organization. For example, some companies have a corporate ombudsman who deals with unethical practices and ethics questions. There may be other company resources available to you.

After reading this chapter you understand what bad bosses can do to you and what you can do. Now list under each of the following bad-boss types what resources are available to you from your organization or company. Include names, telephone numbers and company addresses.

The tough, angry boss

_____

_____

_____

The paternalistic/maternalistic boss

_____

_____

_____

The competitive boss

_____

_____

_____

The deviant boss

_____

_____

_____

Reflections

Summary

In this chapter we've looked at various types of bad bosses and how they can make you look bad and negatively impact your career.

Remember these guidelines when taking action against them:

1. Regardless of the approach you choose, always be able to back up your allegations with facts.

2. Taking assertive action against a bad boss begins by direct, one-on-one confrontation. Spell out what you don't like and how you want to see things change.

3. If that doesn't work, try going over your boss's head, talking to *her* boss.

4. If that doesn't work, try filing a grievance.

5. Public strategies include:

   • Whistle-blowing

   • Legal action

9 GOOD BOSSES: WHAT THEY CAN DO FOR YOU AND HOW YOU CAN MANAGE THEM

If you're working for a good boss, you already know it. Leo Tolstoy once wrote that "Happy families are all alike; every unhappy family is unhappy in its own way."

While not all good bosses are the same kind of people, their effect on their employees can be summed up in a few key phrases. They help you get where you want to go. They take time to listen. They delegate and make full use of their staff's resources. They take chances. They make coming to work fun. They add a sense of purpose and excitement to even the most mundane assignments. They build loyal teams. They're strong leaders, good role models.

In this chapter, we'll look at three kinds of good bosses: Team-Builders, Motivators and Delegators and Charismatic Leaders. We'll also examine what good bosses can do for you, what you can learn from them and how you can manage a good boss.

Why should you take the time to understand your good boss? Because you can learn valuable lessons about managing, team-building and sustaining positive work relationships. These lessons will help you in the future if you become "the boss."

Not all good bosses share the same strengths. It's important to know what makes your boss so great. Is it his willingness to stick up for his employees, his honesty and sense of fair play or his sense of humor? Try making a list of your boss's 10 most valuable characteristics and then prioritize them according to which mean the most to you.

Team-Builders Build Trust

Probably the best qualification your boss can have for being truly outstanding is his ability to build a strong, loyal team. Good team-builders, like good coaches, want players with differing abilities to play specific positions. They know the inherent value in diversity — the more diverse a culture, the greater its strength. Therefore, they don't expect all team members to be alike or play alike. A good manager will take the time to listen to his staff members, get to know each one and learn what motivates each one individually and as part of a team.

What Team-Builders Can Do for You

By working for a good team-builder, you'll learn how to play as part of a team to accomplish a common goal. By becoming part of the process, you become invested in the outcome. The team's goals become your goals.

When introducing a new project, a good team-builder helps you:

- Understand the importance of the project

- Appreciate how your involvement is critical and how you will benefit from the project's success

- Find your own work rhythm

Most importantly, you can learn how individual contributions can be incorporated and transformed into an all-consuming group effort. A boss who is a good coach can get his team to play together by building trust. With trust, groups can gather and process data more quickly and respond to change with greater flexibility.

As a team member, you may also experience more open conflict with team members and with your boss. Yet conflict, based on trust, is honest and healthy. If your boss has built a strong team, it can lead to greater creativity and awareness.

How You Can Manage Your Team-Building Boss

As much as your boss may emphasize the equal status of all team members (including himself), each team also needs a leader — someone they can respect and respond to. To be an effective coach, your boss needs feedback. The more he has fostered an atmosphere of trust, the more honest feedback you can give him.

1. Let him know your feelings and opinions, even when they conflict with his.

2. Let him know if he's dictating his wishes to the team rather than listening.

3. Let him know if he's represented your team fairly to upper-level management.

4. Don't take his criticisms personally.

5. Communicate your appreciation when he rewards the team for achieving a mutually defined goal.

Motivators and Delegators

Good bosses, just like good parents, thrive on knowing they've helped employees grow from employeehood into becoming good bosses themselves. Two ways in which they can nurture development in promising employees is through motivating and delegating.

It's no surprise that bosses who motivate others well are good at communicating their interest in their subordinates. Some companies try motivating employees through incentive programs, bonuses and increased perks. Employees want bosses who care and who take a sincere interest in them, their families and their lives.

At the beginning of this chapter, you made a list of your boss's 10 most valuable characteristics, according to which meant the most to you. Now make a list of your boss's 10 most valuable qualifications as a team-builder — qualities needed to build a strong, loyal team.

1. _____

2. _____

3. _____

4. _____

5. _____

6. _____

7. _____

8. _____

9. _____

10. _____

How is your boss like a coach? _____

_____

Do you feel you can give your boss honest feedback? _____

Why? _____

What Motivators Can Do for You

To truly motivate you, a good boss must also help you develop your talent, use your creativity and push you where you want to go. To do this, a motivating boss can either offer to become your mentor or help you network.

Mentoring, or providing "help from above," is a powerful motivator to succeed. Mentoring can range from giving detailed guidance and advice to general encouragement. It's a wide-ranging show of support given from a person in a powerful position to an employee over a period of time.

A mentor doesn't have to be one's immediate boss. Mentors are some-times bosses in other departments or "experts" in one's chosen field. They can act as good role models, advocates or instructors. Sometimes an employee chooses a mentor, or sometimes a mentor volunteers his advice to an employee. In a few situations the relationship is institutionalized — companies have instituted a formalized structure where aspiring employ-ees can go for executive help.

A mentor can show you the ropes, cut through corporate red tape and introduce you to sources it would ordinarily take you years to find and cultivate. Mentoring is also a way for a boss to groom his replacement.

If, for some reason, your boss can't help you upward, sometimes he can help you move laterally into other bosses' departments or outward into other organizations. This kind of support is called networking.

A good boss who is networking for you is basically selling another potential boss on your abilities: your proven track record; evidence of untapped abilities that would be better used in another department or company; knowledge of your overall goals and career plans; wanting what's best for you.

Networking takes place not only in the immediate workplace but in social settings, within professional organizations and among friends. A good boss recognizes the importance of these connections and uses them to help promising employees get where they want to go.

How You Can Manage a Motivating Boss

The best way to manage a boss who is a good motivator is to succeed. Live the lessons he's teaching you, and show him you're an eager and willing student. Don't disappoint him through unprofessional behavior or laziness caused by thinking you've got it made now that he is helping you.

Motivators thrive on enthusiasm, encouragement and feedback. Use your boss. That's what he's there for. Use him as a role model, a mentor, even as a competitor if that keeps you motivated. The more you show you want to learn, the more he'll teach you.

Bosses Who Delegate

As companies grow, bosses get busier. Good bosses quickly learn the value in delegating responsibility to subordinates. Some bosses have to be pressured into delegating; others seize upon the opportunity. The beauty of good delegation is that it accomplishes several goals simultaneously.

What a Delegating Boss Can Do for You

A boss who delegates well delegates fairly, giving all team members a shot at assignments that can increase their share in the spoils. Delegation also fosters a team's confidence in its leader to prioritize: knowing which projects are crucial, which can be handed around and which call for immediate action.

Once again, delegation is an effective means for a manager to build trust and greater team spirit among subordinates. It shows that the boss trusts those who work for him, causing subordinates to produce more, offer honest feedback and develop into more highly skilled employees.

How You Can Manage Your Delegating Boss

Your delegating boss has shown his confidence in you to do a new job, to take on a new project. His trust is both stimulating and stress-producing. It's a test you don't want to fail, yet perhaps you lack information or expertise to perform with confidence.

Keep the lines of communication open. Your boss has delegated to you not only because he's busy but because he knows you're ready.

Charismatic Leaders

People love a winner. That's because winning is infectious. People like being around highly charismatic leaders because some of their positive energy rubs off.

A charismatic leader can accomplish one very important goal much more easily than other kinds of leaders: obliterating differences and integrating opposing forces into one powerful group.

What a Charismatic Boss Can Do for You

Perform well, and your charismatic boss can do a lot for you. Perhaps he sees possibilities in you that far exceed his own accomplishments. He can tell you what pitfalls to avoid, what seeming shortcuts will only derail your career. To work effectively with his team, a charismatic leader must be accessible to team members; otherwise motivation can quickly fade.

How You Can Manage a Charismatic Boss

Charismatic leaders have to be team players, not just team owners. To be effective, they must also be able to demonstrate they can plan a crusade as well as lead one.

It's not unusual for highly charismatic people to be rather ineffective at detail work, organizing and intensive planning. Find out where your boss's weaknesses lie and then give him badly needed support.

Evaluating Your Boss: Good Manager, Good Leader?

You might not realize it, but bosses are expected to excel in two areas: management and leadership. By learning how to manage your not-so-good boss in these areas, you could turn him into a great boss.

How much you can help your boss depends on how much you're allowed to participate in his decision-making and how well you manage him already. Let's look at the ways in which bosses may carry out their management duties. Evaluate where your boss needs help in the following areas:

Strong Boss — Has It Covered   **Weaker Boss — Needs Some Help**

Managerial Role

Strong Boss — Has It Covered	Weaker Boss — Needs Some Help
Understands his role as manager	Can't distinguish between managerial and non-managerial work
Sees himself as a team leader	Sees himself as THE BOSS
Accepts managerial responsibility	Avoids managerial responsibility
Tries to develop subordinates	Is not concerned with employee development

Duties and Job Knowledge

Always open to new things   Closed to learn new things

Enjoys and understands job   Hates job, doesn't understand

Can handle duties   Job too big

Communications

Accessible   Inaccessible

Initiates   Avoids

Uses a variety of methods   Uses one method

How strong a leader is your boss? Let's look at where your boss could use some help in becoming a more effective leader:

Strong Boss — Has It Covered   **Weaker Boss — Needs Some Help**

Leadership

Praises and rewards employees   Seldom praises

Asks about and monitors employees' progress   Leaves employees alone

Helps employees set goals   Not goal-oriented

Fosters teamwork   Treats everyone on a one-to-one basis

Uses conflict constructively   Avoids conflict at all costs

125

Change

Seeks innovative methods	Maintains status quo
Receptive to new ideas	Discourages new ideas
Expects quick change	Lets things happen slowly
Copes easily with change	Trouble with new procedures

Decision-Making

Flexible	Rigid
Participative	Authoritative
Open	Closed
Enjoys	Avoids

Almost every successful person in business today attributes his style to a good boss who left his impression on that person at some point in his career. The successful boss and the subordinate on his way up often become fast friends because they instantly recognize similar qualities in each other — leadership qualities they both value.

Learn to value a good boss. And if your boss needs some help before he's *really* good, learn to manage him and you'll have a great relationship.

What abilities do you have that your boss can use when he is *networking* to "sell" you to another potential boss?

_____

_____

Assuming your boss is a motivating boss, how can *you* motivate your boss?

_____

_____

What are some ways you can manage your boss when he delegates a new job or project to you?

_____

_____

What areas is your boss ineffective in and needs support?

_____

How can you give your boss support in these areas?

_____

How can you help your boss with his personal goals and objectives?

_____

Reflections

Summary

In this chapter we've talked about good bosses, who they are, what they can do for you and how you can manage them.

You can manage a good boss by:

- Performing your job well

- Being a good team player

- Showing your boss you regard him as a role model

- Giving him feedback

- Sharing your expertise with him

Even not-so-good bosses can become good bosses with the help of supportive employees. You can increase your boss's leadership and management skills by:

- Evaluating how well he knows his job

- Helping him be more flexible

- Keeping him informed

- Supporting his decisions

- Building his visibility within the company

10 TEN WAYS TO MANAGE YOUR BOSS

The importance of learning how to manage your boss can't be overemphasized. In today's busy corporate world, subordinates are becoming increasingly more responsible for maintaining a good working relationship with their bosses. Ultimately, how well you manage your boss will have more direct bearing on your promotability, your current working conditions and your future career moves than your education and expertise.

Here are the 10 commandments for effective boss management:

1. Have a good grasp of your own strengths and weaknesses as well as her strengths and weaknesses. You'll know where you two complement each other, where you conflict and where you need help.

2. Know what she needs — both work needs and emotional needs. When they're legitimate needs such as loyalty, feedback and support, provide them without having to be coached. Never criticize her in front of others. Never underestimate her.

3. Understand the rules of team play. Be willing to be a good team player. Your individual contribution has value, but it's greatly enhanced as a part of the group effort. Help your boss become a good team leader.

4. Learn how to build trust. Show your boss you're trustworthy. Demonstrate your trust in her and she'll come through for you. Let your boss know when she has violated your trust when she has gone beyond the call of duty.

5. Keep the lines of communication open. Give her feedback on her performance. Ask her questions, rely on her guidance. Don't take her criticisms personally.

6. Share your expertise, innovation and creativity with your boss. She can learn from you, too. She relies upon you as a problem-solver and as a source of ideas and skills.

7. Take the initiative, look for solutions to problems and avoid complaining.

8. When problems arise, be straightforward in dealing with them. Develop the confidence and skills to discuss problems with your boss and, if necessary, how you expect her behavior to change. Always stay objective, concise, professional and calm.

9. If your boss is trying to help you, use her as a mentor or networking source. Even good bosses need managing in spots where they're weak. Find out where your boss needs help. Reward her investment in you by performing well. Volunteer for extra projects.

10. Show your boss you understand the duties of management and leadership by incorporating as many of these qualities as you can into your present role. Support her role as manager and leader.

INDEX

A

accusatory review, 104
anger, 30-32
angry boss, the, 58, 60, 104-106
anxiety, 34
anxiety, positive effects of, 37
assessing yourself, 22-27
authorityphilic, 51
authorityphobic, 51

B

biofeedback, use in combating fear, 36
body language, 92, 93
boss-employee friction, 49
bottom-line requirements, 104

C

camaraderie, 102
cardinal rules:
    communicating with boss, 81, 82
    memo writing, 95, 96
chain of command, 6, 7, 12, 13
communication:
    achieving better, 23
    habits, 81, 82
    problems, 86
competitive bosses, 108-110
conflict, resolving, 23
constructive criticism, timing of, 87
constructive feedback, 22
corporate pyramid, 6, 101
credibility, gaining, 70

D

delegating, 19, 24, 119
delegators, 119
dependability, 25
depression, 30, 32, 37, 38
deviant bosses, 110-112
documentation, need for, 105, 106, 109
drug and alcohol abuse, 110-111

E

effective boss, the, 60
emotional crutch, 74-75
emotional demands, excessive, 74-77
emotional needs, determining boss's, 74, 129
emotions, 29-31, 57, 58
evaluating your boss, 124-128

F

family/career conflicts, 22, 23
fearful boss, the, 61
feedback, 22, 56, 57, 61, 87, 93, 119, 130
flattened pyramid, 5
flexible, importance of remaining, 20

G

goals, long- and short-term, 22-25
good bosses:
    effect on employees, 117
    types of, 117
grievances, 106

I

imposter syndrome, 34
incompetent bosses, 100
indifferent bosses, 101-102
information sharing, 65
interpersonal management skills, 101
interpersonal relationships, 21
intimidation, 112

J

joy, effect in workplace, 33
judgmental words, eliminating, 88

L

latent hostility, 31
lateral bosses, 106
lateral move, 121
leader, evaluating, 124, 125-126
legal action, 113
loyalty, 74

M

manage upward, 12
management style, 62-63
managerial role, evaluating, 124-125
meeting follow-up, 95
mentor, 101, 121-122, 130
mentoring, 50
militaristic boss, 62
mission statement, 22
moody boss, 76-77
motivate employees, 54, 60
motivators, 119, 121-122
mundane tasks, 19
mutual expectations, 78, 80, 91

N

network, 121, 130
neurotic bosses, 102, 103
nonverbal clues, examples of, 89
nonverbal communication, 75

O

objectives, 18, 19
obnoxious boss act, 36
one-on-one meetings, 86
overly controlling, 75, 76
overly intimidating, 76

P

paternalistic/maternalistic bosses, 107-108
patronize, 107
perfectionism, avoiding, 57
performance agreement, 94-95
performance measurement, 18
performance review, 73, 104
personal power base, 1
personal style, determining bosses, 62
positive feedback, 73
power:
      of association, 107
      of position, 10, 12, 15, 50, 51
      personal, 10, 13, 51
      pyramid, 5, 6, 15, 50
      referent, 13, 52
      types of, 10
powerholics, 101
preferred lifestyles, 63
priorities, 19
prioritize, 17, 19
proactive, 8, 15, 19
professionalism, 19, 32, 70
psychologically dysfunctional, 77
psychologically powerless, 76

Q

questions to determine:
    effective boss, 60
    how boss expresses anger, 58
    stress in work position, 46

R

rank, 7, 15
recognition, informal, formal, 50
rules, explicit and implicit, 7, 8

S

sabotage, 65
self-management, 18-21
self-trust, 34
self-trust, lack of, 75
setting up a meeting, guidelines for, 91
sexual harasser, 111-112
steps to:
    boosting self-esteem, 33
    building good relationship with boss, 2
    increase boss's leadership, management skills, 128
    managing a good boss, 128
    managing yourself, 18
stereotypical roles, 107
stress, 29, 42-46
subordinates, 1

T

team-builder, abilities, 118
team player, 11, 20, 32, 55
teamwork, value of, 13, 102
time management, 29, 38, 39, 41, 42
tough, angry boss, 104, 105
trust, 33, 34
trust, building, 122
trustworthiness, 64

U

underestimate, 66, 68
unmet work needs, 71

V

verbal abuse, 105
verbal communication, 88
verbal/nonverbal feedback, 93, 94
vindictive response, 88, 106
visibility, 128

W

whistle-blowing, 113

Notes

Notes

Notes

Notes

Buy any 3, get 1 FREE!

Get a 60-Minute Training Series™ Handbook FREE ($14.95 value)* when you buy any three. See back of order form for full selection of titles.

These are helpful how-to books for you, your employees and co-workers. Add to your library. Use for new-employee training, brown-bag seminars, promotion gifts and more. Choose from many popular titles on a variety of lifestyle, communication, productivity and leadership topics. Exclusively from National Press Publications.

DESKTOP HANDBOOK ORDER FORM

Ordering is easy:

1. Complete both sides of this Order Form, detach, and mail, fax or phone your order to:

Mail: National Press Publications
P.O. Box 419107
Kansas City, MO 64141-6107

Fax: 1-913-432-0824
Phone: 1-800-258-7248
Internet: www.natsem.com

2. Please print:

Name_____ Position/Title _____

Company/Organization_____

Address_____City _____ _____

State/Province_____ZIP/Postal Code _____

Telephone (____)_____ Fax (____) _____

Your e-mail: _____

3. Easy payment:

❑ Enclosed is my check or money order for $_____ (total from back).
Please make payable to National Press Publications.

Please charge to:
❑ MasterCard   ❑ VISA   ❑ American Express

Credit Card No. _____ Exp. Date___ _____

Signature_____

• •

MORE WAYS TO SAVE:

SAVE 33%!!! BUY 20-50 COPIES of any title ... pay just $9.95 each ($11.25 Canadian).

SAVE 40%!!! BUY 51 COPIES OR MORE of any title ... pay just $8.95 each ($10.25 Canadian).

***** $20.00 in Canada

60-MINUTE TRAINING SERIES™ HANDBOOKS

TITLE	RETAIL PRICE	QTY	TOTAL
8 Steps for Highly Effective Negotiations #424	$14.95		
Assertiveness #4422	$14.95		
Balancing Career and Family #4152	$14.95		
Common Ground #4122	$14.95		
Delegate for Results #4592	$14.95		
The Essentials of Business Writing #4310	$14.95		
Everyday Parenting Solutions #4862	$14.95		
Exceptional Customer Service #4882	$14.95		
Fear & Anger: Slay the Dragons … #4302	$14.95		
Fundamentals of Planning #4301	$14.95		
Getting Things Done #4112	$14.95		
How to Coach an Effective Team #4308	$14.95		
How to De-Junk Your Life #4306	$14.95		
How to Handle Conflict and Confrontation #4952	$14.95		
How to Manage Your Boss #493	$14.95		
How to Supervise People #4102	$14.95		
How to Work With People #4032	$14.95		
Inspire & Motivate: Performance Reviews #4232	$14.95		
Listen Up: Hear What's Really Being Said #4172	$14.95		
Motivation and Goal-Setting #4962	$14.95		
A New Attitude #4432	$14.95		
The New Dynamic Comm. Skills for Women #4309	$14.95		
The Polished Professional #4262	$14.95		
The Power of Innovative Thinking #428	$14.95		
The Power of Self-Managed Teams #4222	$14.95		
Powerful Communication Skills #4132	$14.95		
Present With Confidence #4612	$14.95		
The Secret to Developing Peak Performers #4692	$14.95		
Self-Esteem: The Power to Be Your Best #4642	$14.95		
Shortcuts to Organized Files & Records #4307	$14.95		
The Stress Management Handbook #4842	$14.95		
Supreme Teams: How to Make Teams Work #4303	$14.95		
Thriving on Change #4212	$14.95		
Women and Leadership #4632	$14.95		

Sales Tax		
All purchases subject to state and local sales tax. Questions? Call **1-800-258-7248**		

Subtotal		$
Add 7% Sales Tax *(Or add appropriate state and local tax)*		$
Shipping and Handling *($3 one item; 50¢ each additional item)*		$
TOTAL		$